How to Dominate a Neighborhood

With Real Estate Farming

Karen Mistrot

Copyright © 2018 Karen Mistrot

www.freshideastraining.com

All rights reserved. No part of this publication may be reproduced or transmitted in any form or by any means, mechanical or electronic, including photocopying and recording, or by any information storage and retrieval systems, without permission in writing from the author.

Disclaimer: The advice and strategies contained herein may not be suitable for every situation. This work is sold with the understanding that the Author is not engaged in rendering legal, accounting or other professional services. The Author shall not be liable for damages arising here from. If legal advice or other expert assistance is required, the services of a competent professional should be sought.

ISBN: 978-1983712142

To my husband Mason and daughter Meredith for putting up with my endless crazy marketing ideas and for the hours spent working on our real estate business.

Table of Contents

Chapter 1: About Me..7

Chapter 2: What is Farming? 11

Chapter 3: Why Farm a Neighborhood?...................................15

Chapter 4: How to Choose a Farm..26

Chapter 5: Should You Live in Your Farm?..............................51

Chapter 6: Rules & Regulations..75

Chapter 7: Beginning a Farm...78

Chapter 8: Many More Farming Examples.............................122

Chapter 9: Resources.. 157

Chapter 10: Summary..160

Chapter 1

About Me

Why in the world would you want to read a book about real estate farming written by me? Primarily, you might want to learn how I was able to succeed in real estate solely by real estate farming. I moved to Colorado in the early 2000's. I was staying home with my daughter while my husband worked his corporate job which involved lots of traveling. I had been in the corporate world myself for about 13 years, but stopped working when we moved to Colorado. I quickly learned that I wanted to get back to work, but I needed some flexibility. I didn't want to travel, wanted to utilize my sales and service skills from my corporate days and I wanted to be my own boss.

I entered real estate without having any background in it. Family members weren't in real estate, I didn't have friends in the business and I didn't know many people in my new town in Colorado. I had bought and sold a few houses with my husband utilizing agents but didn't understand what was involved with being a real estate agent. Sound familiar? How many of us really didn't know what we were getting into until we were knee-deep in real estate?

I succeeded in real estate where many new agents failed

because I knew that I had no friends, family or contacts in Colorado and needed to create my own customer base. I think new agents often obtain their license and just assume that all of their friends and family will start knocking down their door begging for help with their real estate needs. As most experienced agents know, that just rarely happens. Darn it!

With all of this in mind, I started farming. To be honest, when I started farming I had no idea that what I was doing was considered farming. It just made sense to me to market to my own neighborhood. I was consistent with it, tried to be creative with new ideas and provided great service to my clients. Over the years, I became the number one agent of over 3500 homes in my neighborhood for over eleven years. Over the years, I expanded my farm areas and became the number one resale agent in my town for almost five years.

Due to my growth, I was able to create a small team to support my efforts. I was always the rainmaker, or the person that needed to bring in the business. I was the person on the listing appointments and also the person in charge of our marketing. I know many successful agents that have worked themselves out of the listing agent piece and also farm (no pun intended!) out the marketing to someone else. I just never did.

My brand was "out there" – people called me because they knew about my company and that I did a lot of business in my farms. I also "farmed" our past clients and enjoyed a large referral/past client business because of it.

Guess what? All of this was created by real estate farming. Nothing else. No door knocking. No expired calls. No For-Sale-By-Owners. No internet leads. That's not to say you couldn't be successful doing any of these things – I just don't think you have to do them in order to have a successful business. In fact, you could combine door knocking with farming and basically just kick the real estate door in! I personally don't like it when someone knocks on my door trying to sell something so I would not be successful doing it as that opinion would be in the back of my mind while I knocked on doors. I admire those agents that are great at those things – they just aren't for me.

I started teaching farming classes in Colorado to real estate agents because I was receiving lots of calls from agents asking me for help with farming. They either knew of me personally or had heard I was the go-to farming "expert". After having lots of coffee dates, even lots of glasses of wine (even better!) I realized that I should just create a class to address the topic. After teaching lots and lots of agents about farming, I thought it would be helpful to also write a book for agents to use as a reference.

Chapter 2

What is Farming?

Farming is basically marketing to a specific geographic area. The area could be a neighborhood, a city, or even certain streets within a neighborhood. However, I also believe that farming can be applied to groups of people, too. If you have knowledge or interest in a particular group, you might want to try to farm that group. For instance, if you were an accountant in a former life, you might have lots of contacts in that arena. You would also have more information on accountants than the normal real estate agent. Farming the accountants in your city could prove to be quite beneficial. Your background as an accountant yourself might open a lot of doors for you that someone without your background just wouldn't possess.

As I mentioned earlier, I not only farm neighborhoods, I farm my past client database. I also farm local businesses. All are great resources for business. Yes, I need to be creative in how I approach these groups as their needs may be very different. For example, a local business owner may not need to buy or sell a property right now, but guess what? They may very well encounter people every day in their business that do need help with real estate. I want them to think of me when their customers start talking about real estate!

Let's talk a minute about marketing versus advertising. When I market or "farm" a neighborhood, I may use advertising as a farming tool. I also use client events as a tool, social media as a tool, videos as tools and the list goes on. Advertising is just one weapon within my farming/marketing arsenal.

Agents often tell me that farming is outdated or that only "old timers" believe in it. I don't think that is necessarily true and it makes me sad to think that younger agents just discount it immediately. There are so many ways to farm. Digital farming is very popular and definitely works. I can also tell you that when the market was in a downturn around 2007, I still farmed. I was the only agent farming my neighborhoods and while many agents were turning tail and getting out of the business, my business thrived. Was it easy? No. I was living in the land of short sales, foreclosures and clients that were just basically upside-down in their homes. However, they called me to help them as I was the only agent actively farming them!

I know that internet leads are popular with some agents. However, I also know that they are costly and take repeated efforts to get a result. I would make the argument that farming is cheaper and less time-consuming than internet leads. My phone rings because of my farming. I talked to someone maybe two times before I was in their home talking to them about selling. I am not chasing someone down from the internet. That internet lead probably gave me a bogus email or phone number to being with. I am working with people who contacted me and want me to come talk to them, not just anyone who responds quickly. I would rather work with a farming lead all day long compared to an internet lead.

I also think the internet lead world is pretty saturated. It was the "hot thing" for a while. Many companies sprouted up offering the "cleanest" leads at the "best" prices. Personally, I don't want to be available 24/7 and get to talk to someone who may or may not be interested just because I answered the lead at 11 pm at night on Christmas Eve. Do I still get those calls on Christmas Eve? Yep. However, it's a person in my farm who will typically apologize for calling me on a holiday or so late at night. They want to talk to me. I am not chasing them down. They don't expect a call back in five minutes. They are treating my business as a business. That's the kind of business I prefer to be in.

You might think I'm saying that internet leads aren't important. Nothing could be further from the truth. I know many agents who are super successful because they have a system set up to handle the internet leads. I'm just saying that you don't have to go the internet lead route to have a big real estate business. You could do both internet leads and farming and knock it out of the ballpark! I just chose to not go that route. As they say, there is more than one way to do this business. You need to find what works for you and what you enjoy. Success should follow.

Chapter 3

Why Farm a Neighborhood?

I am often asked if farming a neighborhood is really worth the time and expense. My answer is yes and no. Farming is great if you have patience, some creativity, perseverance and are pretty organized. If you possess a couple of these things, but not others, don't worry. You can always hire someone else to be creative or keep you organized! Farming is not great if you want an immediate result or if you don't want to work in a particular area of town – basically, if you prefer being all over town, farming may not be an avenue you want to pursue.

Farming worked for me due to these reasons:

No Need to Travel Far – At the risk of sounding like a lazy agent, I farmed neighborhoods near my home and office. Keep in mind that you don't necessarily have to stay close to home. It just worked for me and my life. At the time I started farming, I had a very young daughter and a husband that traveled a lot. I couldn't show a house across town easily. I had to arrange daycare, etc. I decided that I needed to stay close to home, so I started farming my own neighborhood. Who better than me to sell a house in a neighborhood that I enjoyed living in? A neighborhood where I knew the pros and cons of it like the back of my hand? A neighborhood where I didn't have to think twice about what schools were close by? A neighborhood where I could "preview" listings to see what my competition was doing and also know about those houses when I met with buyers or potential sellers. Let me tell you, I "wowed" sellers when I could provide them details about the house down the street because I had actually been in it! If I was trying to be an agent all over town, I doubt I would be able to preview as many homes. As time went by and my daughter grew up, I could have traveled more. However, I quickly learned that time is money. I didn't want to travel across Denver to a listing appointment in rush-hour traffic for a potential listing that I knew nothing about. Yes, I could do some research on the neighborhood, etc. but if I was up against a farmer, I didn't stand a chance. Plus, at the end of the day was I really the best agent for the seller? Nope. I also liked being able to drive easily to my listings. How many times do you have to just stop by a listing for a second to see something? To meet a contractor? To fill the flyer box? Driving across town to do this for one listing several times in one week just didn't make financial sense to me. If I had someone that really wanted me to help them, but they were far away from me, I referred them to an agent working that neighborhood. It was the right thing to do – for my business, for my bottom line and most importantly, for the client.

I Became the True "Neighborhood Expert" - How many times have you been solicited by a company telling you to send out the message that you are the Neighborhood Expert? I loved going up against those agents because more often than not, they had not sold one house in my farm. When you farm intensely, you know your numbers in the farm. You know which agents are listing houses, which agents are bringing buyers. When I would see a postcard from a so-called Neighborhood Expert, nine times out of ten I would never have heard of them. In addition, their office was often on the other side of town! How could they truly be the expert? By working heavily in my farm, I was the expert. No ifs, ands or buts about it. Before you think "Wow, this lady is full of herself", I'm just saying that I knew my stats, knew my neighborhoods, knew the house issues and knew what buyer hot buttons were in my neighborhood. I couldn't say that about other neighborhoods. I never proclaimed to be the Queen of Real Estate for every neighborhood. In fact, if I listed a home outside of my farm (yes, that did happen!), I would hope that an agent existed that dominated that neighborhood because I would call him/her and ask for assistance. Once I told them that I was going to be a "one and done" agent in their 'hood, they were more than happy to help me. I would go in, sell the house and get out. I didn't want to spend my time or money on a neighborhood that I wasn't farming. Fellow farmers "get it" and typically will always help as they need the sales prices, etc. in their farm to remain stable. They don't want a random agent coming in and skewing the neighborhood stats.

I often just ended up talking to sellers about neighborhood things when I met with them. I wasn't intentionally doing it. It just happened. For instance, I had a listing appointment where I was the last agent in out of five. By the time I showed up, I was impressed that the seller was still willing to meet with me. I don't think I could sit through five listing presentations and I do it for a living! I could tell that she was "done".

I arrived, and she asked if I minded if she rolled out the trash for the next day's pickup. I said I didn't mind at all. I sat down and waited. When she came back, I just casually mentioned how I loved that our neighborhood now had the same trash day. She looked at me with surprise and said "I agree! How did you hear about that?". I explained that I lived in the neighborhood and it always bothered me personally and professionally that every house could have a different trash company and thus a different trash day. On any given day of the week, you could drive through the neighborhood and see trash cans out. Windy days, ugh. You can imagine what the neighborhood looked like. Anyway, in order to get the neighborhood to the same trash day, our HOA had to go through a few years of turmoil. I still can't believe that people became so adamant about keeping their own trash company. The proposed plan saved a ton of money, but people still were hot about the topic and many meetings were held in the neighborhood about trash! Of course, since I farmed the neighborhood, I attended a few of those meetings. Yes, I wanted to roll my eyes many times, but I knew I needed to hear about the trash issues. The seller and I sat down and laughed about those meetings. Ends up that she also attended a couple of the meetings and we reminisced about the crazy antics of some of the homeowners. One thing led to another and we started talking about the elementary school down the street. Her own daughter had attended the school as had mine.

Out of the blue, she said "Okay, that's enough. I want you to sell my house. I want an agent that knows this neighborhood and also loves it. It's been a great neighborhood for me and I want to convey that to potential buyers. Where do I sign?". I laughed and said that we should talk about pricing, marketing, etc. She agreed but said that she had made up mind. Why? Because I knew the neighborhood. I wasn't "faking it". It was genuine. Now, did I care as much when I sold a house outside of my own neighborhood? Of course I did. However, sellers believe that you care more when you live among them.

I Could Direct My Marketing Dollars to a Specific Audience – I admit it. I'm cheap when it comes to spending my business dollars. I am demanding. I want to see a return on investment or I bail. You may have heard the saying – "If you want to sell something, just pitch it to a real estate agent." Agents are bombarded almost on a daily basis by the latest and greatest, the shiniest of shiny objects and we are all tempted. Get business in no time if I just pay for this gadget? I'm there!

I quickly learned that I could go broke quickly if I didn't learn how to manage my business like a business. That's an entirely different topic for a different book, but I knew that I needed to see a return on my marketing dollars. Why else spend the money?

I loved farming because I knew my audience. I knew who the recipients of my marketing would be. I lived in a Denver suburb full of families. Schools were important to them, recreational opportunities were important to them, neighborhood activities were important to them. If I sent postcards out with Happy Hour coupons for a bar in downtown Denver, it would more than likely not resonate with my audience and I would have wasted time and money.

I think agents who put up a billboard or advertise in a city newspaper with a generic message are wasting money. Sure, they are hopefully reaching a lot of people. However, those advertisements aren't cheap either so their cost to obtain a client is pretty high. They are hoping upon hope that their "message" happens to hit home with someone. If I was farming retirees, I wouldn't be focusing on kids' events. Yes, they may have grandkids, but unless they live with them, they would probably not be interested in kids' events. However, maybe I could host a wine and cheese event, hold a seminar on estate planning, etc. I would focus my efforts on my audience and get a better return on my investment.

I Could Easily Start Receiving Those "Come List Me Calls" – This is the best type of call to receive for a real estate agent. I loved it when I would receive calls saying "Karen, I see your stuff everywhere. It seems like you put up a For Sale sign and then it is Under Contract the next day! Can you just come over and tell us what we need to do to get our house on the market?" As great as these calls were, I never took them for granted. It never failed that a long-lost cousin would pop out of the kitchen pantry with her new real estate license. The seller would then say, "I have to use my cousin, or it would create family drama."

That's an entirely different topic, but really? You would risk one of your biggest investments to Cousin Sally with her brand-new license? I know all of us have started somewhere, but I see way too many brand-new agents that think real estate is super easy and that they don't need any type of mentor or supervision. That type of thinking often costs their clients money. But I digress...

Many listing appointments started with the sellers saying "My neighbor said that I had to call you. You know the neighborhood." Those were the best appointments. I knew my farming was producing for me.

It Became More Fun Because I Knew the Area – I knew my farm area inside-out. What I tried not to take for granted was that I knew a lot more than just the geographic area. I knew about past issues with the builders, HOA issues, hot buttons for the homeowners, the most common gripes about the farm area and the reasons that the homeowners love their neighborhood. If I sold a home in a non-farm area, I didn't have all of that information. Many times, I ended up educating some of my sellers about their own neighborhood because they weren't aware of certain things going on. All of this knowledge just made my job not only easier, but much more enjoyable. I knew things and I didn't have to search for information.

<u>I was the "Keeper of the Secrets"</u> – I often learned about things in my farm area that I honestly just preferred to not know about. It was not uncommon for me to go into a listing appointment and be told something that I really didn't want to know. For instance, I have been told in the past that I really should talk to the next-door neighbor because he was going to have to sell his house. Oh, really? Why is that? Well, he was having an affair with Suzie two streets over and their respective spouses were catching on. Okay. I really, really didn't want to know that information. It would never fail that one of two things would happen. One, I happened to know the neighbor or Suzie. Two, if I didn't know them, it never failed that I would meet them within a couple of weeks of learning this wonderful news. I would be shaking his/her hand saying, "Nice to meet you," when in my mind I would be thinking "Oh, so you are having an affair." I didn't like knowing this information (whether it was true or not) because I couldn't get it out of my head.

I would also hear other things about neighbors, etc. People loved to share any and all information that they might have whether I needed to know it or not. Sometimes it was very helpful – Joe was getting a transfer to Pittsburgh and needed to sell his home. Other times it just wasn't nice to hear this stuff at all.

The positive about being the expert for the area and truly knowing it was that I also became the recipient of other valuable information. A commercial developer called me to talk about his plans to build homes in our farm area and wanted my opinion. I often heard things from the Metro Districts or other residents about things that would be going on in the farm. All of this information truly helped my business.

It was a Pipeline for Future Business – This was one of my favorite reasons to farm. It was also one of the things that tested my patience. Every December, my business would slow down. Year after year it would happen. You would think I would remember that it happened every year. Not so much.

A week or two before Christmas, I would always have a mini panic attack. Where in the world was my business going to come from? Why wasn't anyone calling me? Why didn't anyone want to sell their house?

All of those questions were truly silly in my market. Geez,

I often told sellers not to list their home during the holidays. I would recommend listing it right after Christmas. That was a hot time in my market. However, did I listen to my own reasoning? Of course not. I thought that the sky was falling.

However, it never failed. Right after Christmas, my phone started ringing. Sellers were done with the holiday and ready to get going. Buyers had time off for the holidays and actually had sit-down conversations with family and friends about moving. They were ready to buy a house!

How did these sellers and buyers know to call me and not some other agent? They called me because I had consistently been farming them. I was at the top of their mind. They knew who they wanted to call and it paid off for me.

Farming will always be a pipeline for future business if you are consistent with it and don't give up on it too early.

Chapter 4

How to Choose a Farm

Choosing your farm area is by far the most important part of farming. I have talked to way too many agents who don't give this topic much thought. You may hear lots of agents talk about how farming just doesn't work, it's a waste of money and time and that you should try to do something else to generate business.

The odds are good that those agents didn't have success with farming because they didn't choose their farm wisely. When I ask agents why they are farming a certain neighborhood, I often hear one of three responses:

1. I live there. No one knows it better than me and I would love to just work a few minutes from my house.
2. Joe Shmoo is the agent that farms that neighborhood. No one likes him and frankly, I don't know how he does any business at all. He is a jerk and I can do a better job than he does any day of the week.
3. I love the price point. Why wouldn't I want to farm a neighborhood of three million-dollar homes?

All three of those reasons by themselves are NOT the right reasons to farm a neighborhood. Further investigation into the neighborhood is definitely needed. Let me address each one of the reasons and why it doesn't make sense to farm a neighborhood solely based on them.

1. That's great that you live in the neighborhood. You should know a lot about it just by living there. However, does another agent farm the neighborhood? Do many people actually sell their homes in your neighborhood? Is the price point reasonable?

2. We have all known a Joe Shmoo. However, you need to look at Joe's production. Is he successful? If so, he is doing something right. You will have to do even more to surpass his results. That means that you will need to spend more time and more money to make a name for yourself. Is it worth it? Typically, the answer is no. We just have to get past our ego and move on. Go check out another neighborhood that needs a farmer!

3. Yes, we would all love to have tons of million-dollar homes closing. Guess what? Many of them aren't closing all at the same time. They can take much longer to close. Plus, those sellers are typically pretty demanding sellers (not that other price point sellers are not demanding – there are plenty of those out there, too). Are you equipped to handle the sellers' marketing demands? Do you fit with their lifestyle, too? In other words, will you be able to adapt to their needs, questions, etc.?

Choosing a Farm Basics

Can You Relate?

Before you choose a farm, look in the mirror. Would you be able to relate to retirees? Would you feel uncomfortable around young single professionals in a downtown environment? How about families? Would you be able to talk to families about their concerns and really "get" them? You really want to pick a farm area that fits you and your lifestyle.

Relating to a farm isn't necessarily tied to your age. I talked to two male agents about their farming efforts in retiree communities. Let's call them Bob and Tom. Coincidentally, both were in their early to mid-twenties. Both had asked to meet with me to go over their farming strategies. At my meeting with Bob, I was able to figure out why he wasn't successful very quickly. Within a minute of sitting down to talk, Bob started looking at his watch. You've probably met people like this yourself. Keep in mind that Bob had asked to meet with me, not the other way around. Bob's personality was such that he was always thinking ahead. He wasn't fully "in" the conversation.

From my experience with retirees, I have found that they want an agent's time and attention. Many times, these sellers are leaving their homes for not-so-great reasons. Perhaps their spouse passed away or they are moving into an independent living community and aren't happy about it. They want to be able to tell you about their concerns and have you really listen to them. This isn't the case 100% of the time, but it has been my experience most of the time. If Bob was sitting down to meet with them and immediately started looking at his watch, he would be sending a signal that he just wasn't interested in their situation. Bob may actually truly care about these sellers; his personality just isn't showing it. He was not the right match for that farm. Once he came to terms with it and started thinking about another farm that "fit" him, he became excited about farming again.

Tom was in a different situation. He had been farming for five months when we met. He showed me his marketing materials – they were terrific. Tom's farm was a neighborhood that his grandparents had lived in. Tom was close to his grandparents and had spent a lot of time with them. He knew the history of the neighborhood and still knew a lot of the homeowners. He was frustrated because he said nothing was happening and it was costing him time and money. He was about to give up when we met. It ends up that Tom was doing everything correctly. Tom casually mentioned that he had attended a neighborhood event over the weekend and two separate groups of people approached him to thank him for the information that he was mailing to them. Bazinga! I strongly suggested to Tom to not give up. He had to give his farming more time. People were reviewing his information and recognized him, or they wouldn't have come up to him to talk to him. We looked at the number of solds in his farm. They were respectable, but not a ton of homes were being listed each month. His time was coming. I could feel it. He stayed with farming and sure enough, shortly after our first meeting he obtained his first listing. Patience was the key.

Why was Tom successful in this farm while Bob wasn't? Tom's personality. His grandparents had to move out of the neighborhood and Tom was right there beside them and understood their concerns. He had met so many of their neighbors and genuinely enjoyed their company. His age had nothing to do with his ability to successfully farm. His personality completely helped him. He was patient, loved spending time with retirees and understood their concerns.

Choosing a Farm - Numbers

Let's get down to brass tacks. After figuring out if you are a good fit for a farm, you need to next look at the numbers. Numbers never lie in farming.

Total Number of Homes

You will want to find the total number of homes in your proposed farm area. Every area is different, but I could always find my number of homes from a variety of sources. My primary source was my MLS. I had the ability to search by subdivision and a list of homeowners, along with their addresses, would appear. The MLS system totaled the number of homes, so I knew how many houses were in the farm.

A word of warning – sometimes "Happy Valley Ranch" might also be known as other names, too. "Happy Valley Ranch I" or Happy Valley Ranch Annex II". Just make sure that you have included all of the names in your search.

You may also find the number of homes in a farm from your local title company. They will often produce labels for you (typically at a low cost), too. Just remember that you can't re-use the homeowners' names as people move and new people move in. If you are going to use the actual name of the homeowner, make sure it's correct.

The third place that I often would look for the number of homes is the government records. Local government offices are a wealth of information. Many of them can provide the number of homes per community online.

I am often asked what a good number is for a farm. It really depends on your budget and sources of income. If farming is going to be your main source of income, a 100-home farm won't cut it. You won't be able to make enough off of sold homes in that neighborhood to sustain your business. However, if you are looking at a 5,000-home farm, you need to make sure you have the budget and systems in place to farm properly. You can't forget to mail out a postcard. You must have go-to resources to print material, etc. In other words, you need to be organized and prepared. Many times, agents like to start farming a 300-500 home farm to see if it's for them. Not a bad idea!

Let's say for purposes of this exercise that you have discovered that there are 300 homes in Happy Valley Ranch.

Total Number of Homes Sold Per Year

The next number you need to find is the total number of homes sold per year in the farm. Typically, you can find this number in your local MLS. Perhaps you can do a search for "Happy Valley Ranch" along with the category sold. Add in a date range. It should generate the houses that sold during the date range. I used to only look at a couple of years' worth of data. I would now recommend looking at least four to five years' worth of data. It will provide you with a better idea of any type of trend that has happened.

Again, for demonstrative purposes, let's say that you found this information:

Year 1 - 20 Homes

Year 2 - 30 Homes

Year 3 - 15 Homes

Year 4 - 9 Homes

Year 5 - 20 Homes

Calculate the Turnover Percentage

Now that you have obtained both of these numbers, you can determine the turnover percentage. Basically, this percentage will show you how many homes are selling per year in a specific farm.

To discover the number, just simply take the number of homes sold in a farm and divide it by the total number of homes.

For our example, we know that there are 300 homes in

Happy Valley Ranch. We also know how many have sold for the last five years. We just divide number of homes sold per year by the 300, just as I'm showing below:

Year 1 20/300 = 6%

Year 2 30/300 = 10%

Year 3 15/300 = 5%

Year 4 9/300 = 3%

Year 5 20/300 = 6%

How to Figure Out if the Turnover Percentage is Acceptable

You may hear lots of different opinions on what constitutes a good turnover percentage. I personally like a percentage to be in the 6-8% range at a minimum. Does that mean I would not farm a neighborhood with a 5% turnover percentage? Not at all. I use this number as one of the criteria to determine if the farm is feasible. It's an indication of how many houses sell on a regular basis in a neighborhood.

I often talk to agents who really want to farm that multi-million-dollar neighborhood. When they start looking at how many houses actually sell per year, it's discouraging.

Sometimes those neighborhoods have very little turnover. If you are considering such a neighborhood make sure to look at the additional factors before you decide to move forward with farming it.

If you are going to spend time and money on farming, you want to make sure that the neighborhood is one where people sell their houses fairly frequently. If only a couple of houses sell, what are the odds that you would be the agent that they would call? We all know that many homeowners have a relative, best friend, etc. that they feel obligated to use. I would want a bigger chance to be selected so I would want more than two houses selling per year. In addition, will I make any money if I sell only two homes in a neighborhood? Would my expenses be higher than the commissions I would earn?

Make sure to really analyze the turnover percentage before selecting a farm.

Review the Price Point

As I have been saying, some agents only do this step and nothing else. It is an important aspect of determining if a farm is a good one, but it's not the only one. Go to your MLS and search for the sold homes during each of the last five years. Hopefully, your MLS will have an option to provide some stats for those sales. If not, you will have to pull out the old calculator and figure it out.

Once you determine what the average sales price was for the last five years, you need again to look in the mirror and decide if you feel comfortable selling that price range. If it's a higher price range than you are used to selling, are you okay with that? Truly okay. Not okay in the sense that you are saying "Yes, absolutely. I want that higher commission check." Okay in the sense that you are trying to change your business and have plans in place to start selling to higher-end homes. Remember, those sellers have expectations of you spending some money on the latest and greatest marketing. Be prepared.

Perhaps you are tired of having to wait it out with other price points. For instance, maybe a $400,000 house in your town takes a lot longer to sell than a $200,000. Sure, the commission is higher, but you may be spending more to get it sold. Maybe you would like to focus on a higher turnover of sales and want to start farming to lower-priced homes. I see no problem with that thought process.

Overall, just make sure the price point is one that you feel comfortable with personally, that you feel will sell at an acceptable time on the market and that you can handle without a problem professionally.

Check Out Other Agents

This is the last determining factor and again, one of the most important ones. It is also one that most agents just absolutely blow by. Doing so could be a big mistake.

You need to determine if another agent dominates a farm. When I say "dominate" I mean that the agent has a nice market share. Keep in mind it's very hard for an agent to have a 50% market share. It's almost impossible unless it's a new neighborhood and the agent is the builder's preferred agent. To get a 20-25% market share is phenomenal. If you have around 15%, that's very strong, too.

Many, many agents can't get past their own ego. They decide that they can do a better job than Henry Homes. They will say things like "No one likes Henry Homes." Maybe "I don't know how Henry Homes keeps clients or gets business because he doesn't know what he is doing." Another one is "I live in the neighborhood and Henry Homes doesn't. I can do a better job than he does because I live here."

All of those statements are ones that I hear all of the time. Our egos get in the way of smart business decisions. If you look at a neighborhood and see that Henry Homes is basically living and breathing a farm area, it will be tough to overcome his market share. You will have to spend more money and time than he is spending just to get your name noticed. Can you do it? Absolutely. However, I would recommend that you not take that hit financially and time-wise and move on to another neighborhood.

How can you find out if an agent dominates a neighborhood? Numbers don't lie. Go again to your trusty MLS and search for the last five years for the proposed farm. See if you can search by listing agent. If you don't see how, call the MLS. There may be a way. You can then figure out how many homes Henry Homes sold in each of the last years. What is his percentage overall? Take a hard look at the agent's results and determine if you want to try to overcome what he has done.

The next step is to really find out what he has actually done. Search the farm's name and "homes for sales" or something similar on the internet. Does his website pop up? Search "Henry Homes" on the internet. Find out if he shows up in a search sponsoring something for your proposed farm. See if the farm is mentioned a lot with his name. Go to his website – this is a big one. A good farmer should tell you on his/her website that they know the farm. It could be by searches by neighborhood on their site, it could be by having neighborhood news, it could be by showcasing local businesses. You get the idea. If Henry Homes is basically showing that he is the go-to person for the farm, again think long and hard about whether you want to start farming that neighborhood. You will have to do more or be more creative about it.

One caveat about this process. Definitely do this – don't skip it. Yes, you can find out that someone really is dominating a farm, but you may find out that perception is not reality. While I have had many agents tell me that I convinced them not to farm a neighborhood after looking up an agent's information, I have also had agents tell me that they assumed that an agent dominated a neighborhood because they saw his/her advertising or heard others talk about it. Again, numbers don't lie. Maybe the agent is doing a lot of marketing. It may just not be the right kind of marketing for that neighborhood. It could also be that the agent is just getting started doing the marketing. Check things out carefully. You may be surprised.

In summary, get out of your own way. Make a farming decision based on business facts, not personal ones. If you don't, you could lose a lot of money and time. Unless you have tons of both to just blow away, don't do it.

Two Farming Examples

I don't want to belabor this point, but choosing a farm is such an important piece of the entire farming process that I wanted to provide you with a couple of additional examples. Below are two examples of neighborhoods that were analyzed by an agent (me!) to determine if they would be good farm candidates.

Example 1

Neighborhood: Nosy Neighborhood

Number of Homes: 100

Number of Sold Homes:

Year 1 (Most Recent): 9 (9% - 9/100)

Year 2 : 7 (7% - 7/100)

Year 3: 5 (5% - 5/100)

Year 4: 7 (7% - 7/100)

Year 5: 5 (5% - 5/100)

Agent Statistics:

Year 1: Henry Homes 2 (22% - 2/9)

Year 2: Various Agents 1 (14% - 1/7)

Year 3: Various Agents 1 (20% -1/5)

Year 4: Ned Neighborhood 3 (43% -3/7)

Year 5: Various Agents 1 (20% - 1/5)

Average Sold Price:

$350,000

Let's look at these numbers. Remember, numbers don't lie! This is a small neighborhood. As I mentioned earlier, if you are looking to solely farm for your business income, a 100-home farm will not be the right decision. You will need to go to a larger neighborhood. As you can see from this example, only a handful of homes typically sell in a farm of this size. Will you be able to sell all of them? Probably not. If you dominated this farm, you still probably would not make enough to cover your day-to-day expenses and have income left over to live. Bummer, I know!

The overall turnover percentage is not bad. Yes, in Year 3 and Year 5, the percentages were lower than I would like, but overall the percentages are good. I would keep investigating.

When I look at the agent statistics, I see a few interesting tidbits right away. First, it looks like Henry Homes sold a nice percentage of the homes last year even if it equated to only two homes. I wonder if he is starting to farm the neighborhood as he hasn't made an appearance in the previous years. Years 2, 3 and 5 are showing that various agents have each sold one house each. I call them "One and Dones". I was a "One and Done" many times. I would sell a previous client's house in another part of town. They knew that I didn't "know" that neighborhood, but they trusted me to sell the house. I would go in and go out. I had no intention of selling any others in that neighborhood, so I didn't spend any money on marketing.

Many times, you may hear that you should blanket a neighborhood with a Just Listed or Just Sold card for a house in a neighborhood. Yes, you could do that, but know that you are only reaching homeowners twice. The odds of a homeowner needing to sell right when your card arrives is small. However, it does happen. I am just stingy with my money and often won't do that unless it's a high turnover neighborhood that I want to try to get in or if I had great results from my sale and it is close to my home or office. I don't want to drive across town to start up a farm.

Year 4 is interesting in that Ned Neighborhood has shown up. Yes, his solds were several years ago but I would still want to know if he is lurking out there and might make an appearance again.

Overall, I'm just a little curious about Henry and Ned. I would start checking both of them out online. Are their websites indicating that they are the Nosy Neighborhood experts? No, on both accounts. Henry just has a standard issue website by his brokerage. Nothing fancy. Ned has a nice website, but interestingly enough he mentions a couple of neighborhoods across town, not near Nosy Neighborhood. I then search for "Nosy Neighborhoods Homes for Sale". Neither Henry or Ned show up.

The last couple of investigative items I pursue are regarding the actual houses sold. I looked up Henry's homes. They were both on the same street, two houses apart from one another and both sold within a couple of months of each other. I could make the assumption that Henry was in the right place at the right time and that Seller #2 saw the For-Sale sign for Seller #1 and called him or that Seller #2 asked Seller #1 about Henry.

Based on this data, I don't think Henry is a threat to me farming this area. He isn't dedicating himself to Nosy Neighborhood.

Ned is a different story. I started to investigate him a little bit. Interestingly enough, one of the houses he sold in Year 4 was his own. This may sound over the top, but I discover that Ned now lives across town. He happens to be focused on his new neighborhood on his website and is actually doing well with sales in it.

At this point, I would decide that Ned has moved on and isn't interested in farming Nosy Neighborhood any longer.

As for the average sold price, in the market that I am in, $350,000 would be a popular price point for many buyers so I know that I would not have trouble selling that price point. Plus, I have sold many homes in this price range, so I feel comfortable with that number.

What's the verdict? I would farm this neighborhood. All of the numbers are lining up, no agent is trying to farm it and it's at a great price point. Yes, this took a little bit of time to research, but it will pay off. The worst thing I could do is just start farming this neighborhood without any concrete information. It wouldn't make good business sense.

Now on to Example 2.

Example 2

Neighborhood: Awesome Estates

Number of Homes: 933

Number of Sold Homes:

Year 1 (Most Recent): 49 (5% - 49/933)

Year 2: 57 (6% - 57/933)

Year 3: 50 (5% - 50/933)

Year 4: 51 (5% - 51/933)

Year 5: 46 (5% - 46/933)

Agent Statistics:

Year 1: Roberta Realtor 8 (16% - 8/49)

Year 2: Roberta Realtor 8 (14% - 8/57)

Year 3: Roberta Realtor 10 (20% -10/50)

Year 4: Suzy Sales 12 (24% -12/51)

Year 5: Suzy Sales 16 (35% - 16/46)

Average Sold Price:

$1.1 Million

Okay, let's analyze these numbers. They will tell us a story. First, this is a nice-sized neighborhood. When I look at the turnover percentage, it's not super, but again a 5% isn't a reason for me to say completely no to this neighborhood. It's close enough to my acceptable range to be considered. It warrants further investigation in my opinion.

The agent statistics are where the meat of this neighborhood lies. Roberta Realtor seems to have the majority of this neighborhood sales except for Years 4 and 5. I really need to find out more about Roberta Realtor and Suzy Sales, who by the way seemed to be blowing Roberta out of the water several years ago.

Once I started researching Roberta, I discovered that she basically lives, breaths and eats Awesome Estates. I did my online searches and discovered that she sponsors an annual Halloween Carnival, she is a fixture at the neighborhood school, she sponsors a holiday light parade, etc. I also discover that she also lives in Awesome Estates. Hmmm, she is spending a lot of money and time on this neighborhood. I check out her other sales and find that while she does "one and dones" throughout the area, she primarily focuses on Awesome Estates.

Some agents would say "Roberta only sold 8 of the 49 houses last year. There are plenty of other houses for me to sell." That would be a correct statement. However, is anyone else doing as much as she is doing as far as marketing goes? An agent would need to launch a pretty big marketing campaign to get name recognition away from Roberta. Is it worth it?

I also wanted to check out Suzy Sales. What happened to her? Why was she going gangbusters and then disappeared? I looked at her company name. It was Awesome Estates Marketing. Interesting. I then looked at the houses she sold. They were all brand-new homes. Ah ha! She was the agent listed by the builder. She was personally not obtaining these listings from sellers, creating the marketing, and negotiating the deals. Her name was the one being used. Suzy Sales is now working another new neighborhood in another part of town. It appears that there were some new homes in Awesome Estates but the neighborhood is now built-out, so Suzy has moved on. I wouldn't consider Suzy a threat at all to my farming strategy.

Let's take a look at the price point. The final factor. It's a nice one at $1.1 million. Just selling 8 of the 49 houses has created a nice revenue stream for Roberta. I have to figure out if I am a good match for this neighborhood. Would I be able to convince a seller that my marketing is top notch?

At the end of the day, I would not farm this neighborhood. Roberta is doing a good job marketing and she has been able to receive a 14-20% market share. I would say that the average agent doesn't have the time, money or patience to compete with her. Move on!

This is an actual neighborhood in the Denver area. I can't tell you how many times agents told me that they wanted to farm this neighborhood. It was in a popular location and the houses tended to move rather quickly for their price point. Agents were so fixated on this neighborhood that they didn't realize that a newer neighborhood across the street was prime and ready for a new farmer! It consisted of homes that were newer, at the same price point or higher and were in a great location, too. Agents just focused on what they knew and not on what was coming up!

New Construction Neighborhoods

We're at a perfect transition to talk about new construction. Should you consider a new construction neighborhood? Would you run into those Suzy Sales agents and have to compete with them?

I happen to love new construction areas as farm areas - as long as the agent has patience. If you are planning on farming a neighborhood long-term, it can really pay off to farm a new neighborhood. Most people are not buying a home with the intent to sell in a year or two. However, life happens. Job transfers, job losses, divorce, you name it. People's lives change unexpectedly, and homes need to be sold.

Many times, there are no agents farming a new neighborhood. Plus, the homeowners often have purchased the new home without their own agent. They just walked into the sales office and thought about how nice the agent was and decided to basically represent themselves. They don't have a "go to" agent. Finally, if they did decide to hire an agent to help them purchase the home, guess what? Most of those agents finalize the sale and move on. They don't stay in touch at all.

So who would come to mind when the new homeowner needs to sell? They usually go back to the sales office and ask for a referral. What a huge opportunity for an agent! If you would start farming a new neighborhood and get in on the ground floor, you could "own" that neighborhood farming-wise down the road. What a great time to obtain the original floorplans from the sales office, to learn about the building materials used, what schools the neighborhood feeds into, etc. Who knows? You could also pick up some buyers just because you are so focused on this neighborhood and are the expert at it.

There is one big caveat with this idea. You won't make a ton of money overnight. As I've said before, farming is not an overnight, get-rich-quick scheme. It's a business plan for the months and years to come. With new construction, it could be even longer. The standard rule of thumb is that most people sell a house every five to seven years. I'm sure it may be different in your neck of the woods. However, that's the number nationwide. You may capture some of those people who have to sell unexpectedly. However, what you are really going for are the people that will start selling in 5-7 years. Getting in on the ground floor really provides you with a wealth of knowledge that agents trying to farm an established neighborhood will never have an opportunity to obtain.

So...if you have the patience and desire, go for it. Farm that new construction neighborhood!

Chapter 5

Should You Live in Your Farm?

Spoiler alert! I lived in my farm and was successful, so my answer is going to be "yes" in this section. However (and that's a BIG however), I sure wish I knew some things before I started farming in my own neighborhood. Let me state right here: you **do not** have to live in your farm. Again, you **do not** have to live in your farm. It's one of those real estate myths that are just "out there" and people assume the myth is a fact. Many successful farmers do not live in their farm.

What would be the Pros of living in a farm? There are several in my opinion.

Pros of Living in Your Farm

No Need to Travel Far

My first pro is that you don't have to travel far at all. I seldom ever used my GPS. I knew the streets of my neighborhood. I could easily get to a listing appointment from my house or come home after an evening appointment within five minutes. It was terrific. I talked to many agents who were trying to be all things to all people and driving across Denver in the snow in hopes of getting a listing appointment in a neighborhood that they really knew nothing about.

While I may sound like I was a lazy agent not wanting to travel far, that's the farthest thing from the truth. In fact, the old saying "time is money" comes into play for this one. I knew driving across town to go to a listing appointment that I probably spent much more time preparing for than a "farm" listing appointment was not a good use of my time. If I was up against an agent that lived in the area, that "knew" the neighborhood better than I did, etc., I didn't stand a chance. I would rather spend my time on more productive things in my business and generate more business in my farm.

Did I ever go to listing appointments outside of my farm? Absolutely. They were typically past clients or referrals. If there were extenuating circumstances, I was there. However, I never once pretended to be something I wasn't. I never told customers that I sold homes in their neighborhood if I had not done so. One, that's not ethical. Two, I knew it would become apparent that I didn't have much information on the neighborhood as we walked through the transaction. Not a great feeling for the client.

In a nutshell, driving across town in traffic or snow was not my idea of a productive use of my time. Some agents say that driving relaxes them. Maybe on a nice country road! However, I would still argue that they could be using that drivetime there and back so much more productively.

Easy to Become Involved

My second pro is that living in a farm made it pretty easy to become involved with the farm. It probably sounds kind of obvious, but you may be surprised at the number of "secret agents" that are living in neighborhoods. I know many agents that just live in their homes. They don't engage with their neighbors, their schools, activities in the neighborhood. They don't use the amenities that might be available. I get that. Sometimes you just want to live peacefully and be invisible. If I am describing you, you may not want to farm your own neighborhood unless you are willing to change.

Becoming involved in the neighborhood should be relatively easy if you haven't kept your head in the sand while living in your home. Many neighborhoods have activities that are sponsored by the HOA. If a neighborhood doesn't have activities, what a huge opportunity for you! You can create your own! If there are current activities, reach out to the person in charge and see if there is something you could do to help.

When I started farming, as I said I didn't know that what

I was doing was actually called farming. I didn't have a great plan of attack. I remember in September thinking "Hmmm, I know our neighborhood always does a Fall Festival. I wonder if I could donate kids' drinks or something." I had been to these Fall Festivals in the past prior to my realtor life. I knew what they were like and I remember that my own daughter would have enjoyed being able to have drinks available.

I reached out to the person in charge of the event (yes, this took me awhile to figure out who the right person was) and asked if I could donate drinks. I was met with an overwhelming "yes!". She then said that I could set up a table or tent with information if I wanted to do so. Today, I wouldn't dream of volunteering drinks at an event without an expectation of having a table or tent with my information available. At the time I had asked, I was surprised with her response, but immediately said "Sure, I'll be there!". Of course, I had to rush around and try to get a banner, buy a table, buy the drinks and then figure out what I was going to give away at the event to be memorable in residents' eyes.

Long story short, I worked with that contact for years. I became a "go to" if she needed a sponsor and I often asked her if I could sponsor other things. I always told her if I was going to host a neighborhood event, too. I could do that without the HOA approval, but I wanted to make sure to keep her in the loop.

It's easy to get involved in your neighborhood since you should have access to information telling you what is happening on a regular basis. Just think out of the box for a bit and figure out how you could help the HOA but at the same time, promote your business. Become the "go to" resource for your neighborhood HOA!

You "Know" the Area

Again, this might seem like one of those "duh" comments but think about it. You live in your neighborhood. You drive around it. You have noticed when a road is closed, when a business has shut down, when something is being built. You "know" the neighborhood. For a neighborhood that is across town, you may not know a thing because you are never over there. This type of information is invaluable.

You can easily describe a listing as being within walking distance to "Kiddie Acres Elementary" because you know that it really is close to the school. I listed a non-farm home once and had no idea that a big recreation center was nearby. Should I have known? Yes. I should have scouted out the neighborhood and figured it out. However, I wasn't familiar with the roads around the house. I happened upon the recreation center and went "whoa!". It was impressive. My sellers never mentioned it to me because they weren't into a recreation center. However, potential buyers might have been. I should have used this information in my marketing but didn't because I didn't know about the recreation center. Yes, the house still sold and for a great price. Could it have sold faster? Perhaps it could have if I had known more about the neighborhood.

You Become Recognizable

I'll give you a warning. This one is both a pro and a con. I'll talk about the pro portion right now and get to the con later.

I branded myself pretty early on. I had my photo on everything. Was I really that vain? Absolutely not. I just wanted to be recognizable. Real estate is a very personal thing for many sellers and buyers. By putting my photo on my signs and marketing, people felt like they knew me when they may never have met me.

I actually ended up opening my own brokerage. Before I did so, I talked to several other brokerages about possibly joining them. For various reasons, I chose not to do so. Interestingly enough, I was very close to joining a brokerage with some terrific agents. I really liked the "feel" of the agency and their business practices. I had a great deal of respect for many of their agents. What ended up being the deciding factor was that they would not allow me to have my picture or my website on my sign. They had branded themselves as a company and wanted everyone to have the same sign around town. To this day, they still do that, and I still think that is a mistake on their part. I have learned that clients are not buying the real estate company, they are buying the agent. Sellers want to know if the agent has their best interests in mind, how he/she will market their home, what systems do they use, do they connect with him/her and on and on. No one looks at only "XYZ Company" listings. Buyers look at everyone's listings, so it doesn't benefit a seller to have only a "XYZ Company" agent in order to bring in buyers. Ultimately, sellers are choosing an agent based on the agent, not the company. Buyers are choosing a house based on the house, the location, price and marketing done for the home. Neither sellers or buyers are choosing an agent or home based on the company for which they work.

I digressed, but I think it's an important point to make. Brand yourself. Let people in your farm know who you are. I attended HOA meetings, school meetings, neighborhood events. I was seen in the neighborhood. You might not realize it, but people notice if you are in attendance. You are showing that you are part of the community and care about it.

A grocery store was located in the middle of my farm. The joke in my family was that I couldn't go into the grocery store and get out quickly without seeing someone I knew. It could be someone that felt like they knew me from my marketing, it could be a listing prospect that I had met with or even a buyer of a listing from years ago. I was stopped and asked about the real estate market in general or about a house on their street. You name it. I was recognizable.

You literally become a mini-celebrity in your own neighborhood. My ego never did get too big because I could easily drive 5 miles to another grocery store and walk in with no problem at all. No one recognized me!

You Hear Things

Since I lived in my neighborhood, I heard about things that I never would have known about if I had lived somewhere else. For instance, neighbors talked about other neighbors, schools, amenities, etc. Just living in the neighborhood provided me with a wealth of information.

I would often joke that I had a few detectives on the payroll. Lots of people would call, text or email me with information. They thought I might want to know some things. For instance, did I know that "XYZ" restaurant was probably going out of business due to tax liens? Had I heard that the principal at the community elementary school was not well-liked? What was going on with the lifeguards at the pool? The list goes on and on. In one way or another, this information became valuable to me as I truly became an expert in the farm.

Neighbors also would tell me when someone would probably be selling their home. I would often be told that Joe or Jane might be getting divorced or being relocated. I also heard if someone who chose another agent was happy with that agent. Legally, I couldn't (and wouldn't!) contact a seller if they were working with another agent but my neighbors sure did. I would get business from neighbors telling other neighbors that they should have gone with Karen and their house would be sold. If the sellers' house was not sold when the contract with the listing agent was expired, I would often receive a call. Almost one hundred percent of the time, I had no idea that neighbors had been talking about me with the sellers. Total surprise, but a very nice one!

In other words, just by living in your farm, you will become a treasure trove of information about the farm.

Your Credibility is High

When you live in a neighborhood and have a listing appointment in it, you automatically have an advantage. Some agents just casually mention the fact while others say nothing. They don't want their clients to know that they live down the street! Huge mistake.

When I conducted a listing appointment in my neighborhood, I always made sure that the sellers knew I lived there and for how long. I wanted them to know how involved I was with the neighborhood – what I supported, what I sponsored, what schools I donated to, what events I participated in, you name it. You automatically become a true neighbor to the seller. If you just moved to a neighborhood, I would focus on how excited you are to live in the neighborhood and how much research you did before you decided to move into the neighborhood. Hopefully, you really did that research as any good agent would do. You may end up passing on some information that the seller doesn't even know! Even if a seller is moving out of the neighborhood because they absolutely can't stand the area, they will still want to hire an agent that truly loves the neighborhood. They will feel like that agent would share that information when talking to other agents and buyers.

Many sellers find comfort in the fact that an agent lives in the same neighborhood. They think that the agent can stop by easily when needed and will want the highest price possible for the house since he/she lives in the neighborhood. I was often asked by sellers if I had buyers for their home. I often knew of some because I would receive calls from buyers looking in the farm. They knew that I did a lot of business in the neighborhood and that I might hear about houses coming on the market. This was a definite plus on my side at a listing appointment.

I can't tell you how many times sellers would tell me that they wanted to hire an agent that "knew and cared" about the neighborhood. Does this mean that only agents that live in a seller's neighborhood can do a good job selling a house? Absolutely not. I would argue on the anti-farming front that a good agent could overcome a farming agent if he/she has a killer listing presentation, truly researched the neighborhood, knows the numbers inside and out and can articulate well what he/she can provide to the seller. Just because an agent farms a neighborhood does not make them a great salesperson. Several times, I won non-farm listings over a neighborhood farming agent because that agent just didn't "wow" the seller. He/she assumed that they would obtain the listing because they lived in the same neighborhood.

When a terrific listing presentation is combined with a sharp agent that lives in the neighborhood, that agent will almost always win the listing. Yes, even if the agent charges more. A very good agent would be able to explain how he/she would actually net the seller more money than a low-priced agent because of the neighborhood knowledge and skills that the agent possesses. Another topic for another book, but it's very possible for a well-prepared farming agent to win a listing over a "low cost" agent.

Overall, if you live in the neighborhood and are a good agent, your credibility will be higher than an agent that doesn't live in the same neighborhood.

Let's move on to the Cons of living in your farm. Unfortunately, some definitely exist.

<u>Cons of Living in Your Farm</u>

When I started farming, I sure wish that I had done some research or perhaps read a book like this one. I really don't think a good farming book existed at that time, so it might be a moot point. There are some definite cons to living in your farm. Really, truly look at these Cons and determine if you (and your family) are okay with them. If any of these bother you, think about farming another area. It could be close by, just not right by your own home!

You are Never "Off"

Wow. When I started farming, I never thought about this one piece of it. When I was working in the Corporate world, I would work long hours and travel. However, when I came home, I was home. When you farm a neighborhood that you happen to reside in, you are never "off". It was not uncommon for someone to show up at my doorstep (always during dinner) and want to talk about a listing down the street. Why did I list the house for that price? Would it be possible for that person to get more for their own house? Oh, by the way, their cousin would be listing their home, but they knew that I "knew" the neighborhood and wanted a professional opinion. You don't have to farm to get those type of questions (gotta love those people that want your expertise, but don't want to pay for it), but you probably won't have them show up at your front door.

I also quickly learned that I couldn't walk on the walking paths in our neighborhood without getting stopped by someone wanting to talk about real estate. Yes, that's what we want, right? For me, I needed a break every now and then. I ended up not every wanting to go walking, at least not where I lived.

The neighbors on our street would sometimes wait until I pulled into our garage to run up the driveway to "catch" me to ask me some real estate questions. I don't know about you, but sometimes I was in a hurry or running late to do something and didn't have time to talk. I actually had people flag me down on the street while I was driving and ask me to roll down the window so that they could talk to me.

Basically, your neighbors may very well not have any boundaries. They see you as "Happy Valley Ranch" Real Estate Expert. If you are getting a new roof, uh oh, you must know something. Should they be getting a new roof? If I painted my house a certain color, was that a "hot" color? Should they do the same thing?

My farm had some terrific amenities. Unfortunately, in my last years of farming the neighborhood, I seldom utilized the pools. I could not go to the pool and just relax or talk to friends. People would see me and ask if I was "Karen". They would then want to talk real estate. I was often told that so-and-so saw me at the pool at 5pm on Sunday. I may not even know "so-and-so". The topper was when sellers would see me at the pool and wonder why I wasn't working on selling their house. Just not worth it to me.

As I said earlier, overall never being "off" was worth it to me professionally. However, on a personal level, it was exhausting at times.

You Become Recognizable

This is what every agent aspires to be – recognizable. You want to be known as the go-to person for real estate. Again, being recognizable definitely was a positive in my business. Unfortunately, it came at a personal price.

As an example, when my daughter was small I would attend every event at her elementary school (okay, so yes, I attended every event throughout her school years). In her elementary years, my husband had not joined the real estate team yet. He was in the Corporate world and traveling often. He tried really hard to be present for school events, dance competitions, sporting events, etc. However, as is often the case, the Corporate world really didn't care if an elementary school talent show was occurring. He had to miss a few things. I would attend the event, making sure to arrive early to get a good spot to record the event. I was by myself as we didn't have family here. If I didn't show up, my daughter would not have anyone there in attendance. I would record it and we would have a "movie night" of sorts when he returned so he could watch it.

My daughter's elementary school was dead-center in my

farm. Lots of pros with that fact. One big con was that the other kids' parents were potential or current clients. Many of them had the "no boundary" issue. More times than I want to think about, I was pulled aside to talk about real estate. No, it wasn't because they wanted to sell their house or even knew someone who wanted to buy. It ranged from the standard "Why did my neighbor's house sell for XYZ?" to "Could you tell my neighbor to trim their bushes? They have been bothering me for a long time and since you know everyone I thought that you could mention it to them."

At the beginning, I talked to them. Sure, no problem. I'll go out into the hall to talk to you. Don't worry if I miss my daughter's performance, time on stage, etc. I guess you really don't care if you miss your own child's time on stage. After doing this a few times and being so angry that I missed my daughter performing or whatever it was at the time, I realized that she was also very upset and disappointed. Her face would fall and she would say "that's okay". At that point, I drew the line in the sand. No more. I would never get those times back. I would politely say "Sure, I would be happy to talk to you after this event. I really am here to watch Meredith do "xyz". How about if we talk afterwards (not the perfect solution as my daughter would be waiting on me) or maybe I could reach out tomorrow?"

Boy, I angered some people. I had someone say that I must not be "hungry enough". Killed me. I pride myself on my work ethic. No one is going to out-work me. I tried very hard to work smarter, not harder. However, my family came before work. When people interrupted an event, they wanted to talk to me right then and there. They didn't have any consideration for my personal time. I had to come to terms with the fact that I didn't want to work with people like that and if I found that out earlier than later, then that was a good thing.

My car became recognizable, too. I didn't have a fancy-dancy car that was one-of-a-kind either. I was fortunate to have nice cars, but they weren't flashy. I never "wrapped" my car. Many agents believe strongly that their own car should be flamboyantly marked as "Judy J. – The BEST Real Estate Agent Ever!". Sure, it would have been powerful to have my car being seen everywhere in the farm. However, I can't tell you have many times I met with sellers who wanted me to keep our conversation confidential. They didn't want anyone to know that they were thinking of selling their home.

I will always remember one of my listing appointments. I was meeting with a woman about selling her home. Her phone was next to her and started ringing. She looked at it and said "Hmmm. I should answer this – it's from my neighbor across the street. She doesn't call often." I said to go ahead. Ends up that the neighbor wanted to know if she was selling her house because she saw "Karen's car" in her driveway. The seller became angry and accusingly asked me if my car had my name all over it. I said absolutely not. We even had to look out the front window, so she could see the proof. She calmed down, but I would have been escorted out at that moment if I was advertising that I was at her house. The neighbor? I knew her from my daughter's school and she had seen my car. Again, it was a basic SUV. She must have been watching out the windows of her house and knew when the car pulled up at her neighbor's house that I was visiting. This type of situation happened more than once. Sellers often want you to be discreet.

My last example of never being "off" involved my daughter again. She was a Girl Scout. In our neighborhood, selling those cookies could be very competitive. The Girl Scouts had to be out there the first day that they could sell those cookies because if they waited, another girl would have already sold to the street. So my daughter would be ready for that day. In Colorado, it never failed that it would be about zero degrees, too. I would go with her because I just didn't feel comfortable with her knocking on strangers' doors. I would stand out on the sidewalk and let her do her thing at the door.

It was not uncommon that several times people would see me and start asking real estate questions. "Oh, Karen, do you think you could come in and take a look at our basement? Can you tell if our house would sell with what we did?". "Is that you, Karen? Hey, can we talk about what a good price for our home would be?". So I would go inside, and we would take off our coats, boots, gloves, all of the cold weather paraphernalia. My daughter's face would fall, and she would look outside and sometimes see other Girl Scouts across the street selling! Needless to say, I was fired by my own daughter. She needed her dad to sell with her. Nothing personal, just business. Ha!

Being recognizable in real estate is what agents strive to achieve. Just be aware that it comes with a price in your own neighborhood!

You Become the Complaint Department

This Con is amusing to me. At the beginning, it was an irritation, but I quickly turned it into an opportunity to chuckle. Everyone needs a good laugh.

For whatever reason, if you are a successful farmer, you will become a Complaint Department. Before I entered into real estate, I don't think I ever called a real estate agent once to complain about a neighborhood issue or even ask a neighborhood question. The fact that people did it to me on a regular basis still floors me to this day.

Some questions that I fielded were "normal". What time does the pool open? Who is the principal of the high school? Who plows the snow on the neighborhood streets? I answered each and every question or found the answer and called them back. I didn't mind. I wanted to be a helpful resource for the neighborhood.

The complaints outweighed the other questions. Let me give you come examples. Why doesn't Joe Shmoo pick up after his dog when he is walking it? Why isn't the mulch being replaced at the pool? It needs it! Why did the landscapers not cut the grass a certain way behind my house? Why are there so many mosquitos around the retention pond and can you make sure it gets sprayed because we are getting eaten alive? Can you call my neighbor and ask him to shut up his dog? He barks constantly. I don't want to be in a bad relationship with him. Why is the HOA giving me grief over parking cars in front of my house? Who called them to complain? I could literally write another book about all of the complaints and questions that I received.

I answered every question and complaint. Did I go over

and tell someone to keep their dog quiet? Absolutely not. However, I provided resources for people to handle it themselves. Yes, that's not what they wanted most of the time. They wanted to really dump the problem in my lap. I wouldn't take those on. Adults needed to act like adults. Hard concept for some to understand, I know.

One of my favorite examples was regarding a woman that called me. She explained that she lived on a certain street. I happened to have a listing on that street and had recently sold a couple of others. I thought she initially was calling me because of those things. Nope.

She started the conversation by asking if I knew where a certain plot of open space was located. Yep, I was familiar with that area. I had been to it numerous times. She asked if I knew that white circles were now located on the open space. I did not know about the circles. She asked me why they had been painted. I had no idea, but I told her that I would see what I could find out. She thanked me profusely and said that she knew she should call me because I would help her.

I proceeded to try to find out the answer. It actually ended up taking a while because it involved government offices. First the HOA. No idea. Strange, but okay. Then the

County (the farm was out of the town's limits). One department didn't know who would know so they transferred me to someone else, etc. You get the idea.

I called the lady back and told her that I was working on it, but had not found out an answer yet. She was very appreciative for the call and said she would be patient. After finally receiving the answer, I called the lady. I explained that the County said that the lines were painted for aerial survey purposes. She was so relieved. She said that she had told all of her neighbors that she had called me to find out the answer and that she just knew that I would find out. Guess why she was so upset? Get ready. After she told me that she made sure to tell all of her neighbors that she would get to the bottom of it because she had called me, she proceeded to tell me that she was afraid to take her little dog Dixie over to the open space for walks and Dixie loved that area. I told her that it sounded like it would be fine to take Dixie back to the open space. She was ecstatic. She said that she was certain that the circles had been created by aliens to indicate the pick-up spots of humans and their pets. She thought that she and Dixie would be transported to another planet if she happened to be in the open space when the aliens were nearby.

After she explained this to me, I think I was probably

quiet for about 30 seconds. I thought that I had heard everything. I kept thinking "Wow, that took some time to figure this one out and that's why I did it?". However, I quickly reminded myself that I not only helped ease this woman's mind, but that I knew she would go tell all of her neighbors what I did. I wasn't looking for praise, but I did want to be known as a resource for the farm. I was hoping that her neighbors were thinking the same things that I had been thinking such as "Was this woman serious?". When they heard that I took the time to research her concerns, maybe they would remember that when the time came to find a true neighborhood real estate expert!

In a nutshell, just be prepared for some of these calls, both "normal" and the "not-so-normal"!

You Hear Everything

I talked about this earlier, but a farmer hears almost everything in the neighborhood. As I said, sometimes it is very valuable information about houses potentially selling, maybe it's something going on with the HOA, sometimes it's about the schools.

Many times, I heard things that I just didn't want to know about it. I heard about police coming to neighbors' homes for domestic violence accusations or because the kids were in trouble for drugs or vandalism. People just wanted to share this information. I heard about divorce details that I really didn't need to know about.

I would negotiate a deal for a listing in the neighborhood and perhaps the buyers were adamant that they wanted a financial credit, so something could be fixed in the house. Guess what? I would drive by that house numerous times and notice that a contractor was never present or that the item had never been repaired (if it had been outside). If I didn't notice it, I would often hear from the neighbors saying how the new buyers were bragging that they took the money with no intention of doing the repair, etc. Ugh. How ugly and frustrating. I'm not saying that happened every time and yes, I know that's a risk with any real estate transaction. It just didn't make me feel really good when we operated in good faith.

I know that there is gossip in any neighborhood. It's part of life. It's just different when it bleeds into your business life. I not only knew more than I wanted to know about my neighbors, but those neighbors often were clients, too.

It was very common for me to hear this kind of stuff on a daily basis. Just be aware that you will truly become a "Keeper of Secrets" if you live in your farm!

Chapter 6

Rules and Regulations

I would be remiss if I didn't mention that every agent should be well-versed in the rules and regulations of not only his/her state's real estate department, but of his/her local MLS organization.

For instance, when I advertised in my farm, I had to know what disclosure statements I needed to provide. On almost every marketing piece I indicated "If your home is currently listed with another agent, please do not consider this a solicitation". I often would mail items "bulk mail" which meant that it was not addressed to a specific person, but instead to a house address. I would mail to every address in a "route code". I couldn't pick and choose which homes to include and which homes not to include. The route codes for the most part were organized neighborhoods so that was helpful. However, I could be sending a marketing piece to a homeowner who had their home listed with another agent. In my state, that could be considered "solicitation". I could be viewed as trying to take the listing away from the current agent which was not allowed. By putting that disclosure on the piece, I was indicating that I truly was not trying to obtain that business.

Many states also have rules about teams. Your state may mandate that your brokerage name be very visible on marketing pieces along with your team name. Maybe your state won't let you use the team name. Maybe your state has rules about the font size on your marketing pieces. Be aware of the rules. Learn them and use them. Don't make a mistake or it could cost you a fine or perhaps a censure from your state. It just takes one agent to turn you in and guess what? It appears that there are agents out there that love to turn in other agents. Don't give them a reason to turn you in.

I would also check out the rules and regulations about advertising sold properties. I often received marketing pieces from agents with pictures of homes that had sold, along with the sold price. They were saying that they were the "Neighborhood Expert" on the marketing piece. Since I lived and breathed my farm, I knew that the houses were not listed by the agent nor did they bring the buyer. It was very misleading to the public as they would assume that the agent was the actual agent that sold those homes. In our state, we had to disclose if we actually sold the house. If not, we had to indicate that we didn't sell it.

I also had to make sure that I indicated where I was getting the information that I was providing on my marketing pieces. Was it from the local MLS? Another website? I had to inform the consumer as to where the information was obtained. My MLS also had a disclosure that I needed to print basically saying that they couldn't be liable for the accuracy of the information. Makes sense as agents were the ones entering the data and sometimes mistakes were made upon data entry.

The last item that I will mention is to make sure that you know the rules about how old the sales that you report can be in your state. Basically, can you advertise a home that you sold in your farm five years ago? We could only go back three years. Again, it was to protect the consumer. Maybe an agent sold several houses in a neighborhood and then moved away for five years. The agent came back and started advertising that he sold all of these houses, but it was more than three years ago. I don't know about your real estate market, but in three years my market could have changed dramatically!

Chapter 7

Beginning a Farm

Okay, you have now read why you might want to farm, you have discovered a neighborhood that you would like to farm and have decided if you want to farm your own neighborhood. With all of that in mind, you have decided that yes, farming is something that you want to try. Where should you start? I have several ideas to share. Some are absolutely free which is important if you have a small budget or maybe no budget at all. Other ideas will take money, so I am only going to mention ideas that have worked for me.

Set a Budget and Stick to It

Before you start to farm, this is probably one of the most important things to review. The school of thought is that you should spend about 12-15% of your Gross Commission Income on marketing. Since I farmed solely, that would mean that my entire marketing budget was going towards farming. Personally, I think that 12-15% is kind of high. I was cheap and pretty demanding with my marketing money. I wanted to see a return on my investment. The highest number that I ever used was 10%. I typically tried to fall in the 8% range. I could sleep at night using that number.

By setting a budget upfront, you know what you are

willing to spend. If you are a brand-new agent, figure out what your Gross Commission Income goal is for the upcoming year and use that. Be realistic. I don't want to be a downer, but we would all like to make that million-dollar commission income our first year in real estate. It's just that not many agents can reasonably do that.

Let's say that last year's Gross Commission Income was $50,000. I like to use round numbers for examples if possible. You sure hope to make more in the coming year, but you know what you made this past year and are planning on doing at least the same amount again, hopefully more. Take that $50,000 and multiple it by maybe 10%. You now have a $5,000 marketing budget for the upcoming year. If you are brand new and are estimating that you will make $50,000, use that $5,000 number, too. However, if you don't have that money in reserves, don't use that for your budget. Only use the money that you actually have. You should not be going into debt to farm. Don't take out a loan to obtain your marketing budget. There are some free things you can do that might generate income for you. Just make sure to set aside some of those commission checks for future marketing expenses the next year.

I would always create a marketing budget and calendar in November for the next year. My business tended to slow down in November and December and it was a great time to reflect on what worked, what didn't, what I wanted to do the next year, etc. By taking the time to do this, your marketing will happen without you having to sit down and come up with new marketing ideas every so often. In the busy times of real estate, taking the time to market is often not a priority to agents. When it starts to slow down, they often say "Wow, I wish I had marketed this past summer! What was I thinking?". Well, they were probably trying to focus on the actual business of real estate and didn't have time to come up with a marketing plan. By doing it in the slowest time of the year, you have made your life much easier for the coming year.

When planning for the upcoming year, have a big calendar out in front of you. Plan how you are going to stay in front of your farm each month. For example, if you are going to do a monthly newsletter, write down the publication date for it each month. After the "newsletter" caption, put the amount it will cost you to do it. You will be able to see easily how much you are going to spend each month on that newsletter.

You will need to also have that newsletter created. Put that on your "to do" list. Make sure it pops up every time you need to start working on it. Some people farm out this piece (no pun intended). If you do that, make sure that's on your "to do" list– "Notify Suzie to get the newsletter to me by the 10th" or something like that. By having a "to do" for every step of the marketing and the budget dollars next to them, you will be able to see at a glance what you are doing each month. You may need other "to do's". Perhaps, "revise newsletter", "print newsletter", "deliver newsletter" – think of every step that needs to be done so the newsletter actually does get finished and mailed on time!

Another benefit of having a budget is that it makes you stay honest. If you have been in this business any length of time, you know that it appears that everyone wants a piece of your paychecks. Your office, your MLS, your contract software program, your E & O insurance – and those entities are just the ones that you must pay in order to stay in business! You also will receive tons (and I do mean tons) of phone calls, emails and texts from every vendor out there. They will try to sell you the latest and greatest marketing tool to increase your business. Boy, some of them are ridiculous, but agents are buying them because they wouldn't be calling you if someone didn't say "sure" once or twice. Others really look like they have potential and you will be so tempted to buy them. You will have an agent friend who swears by them. If you have a budget and stick to it, you can easily say to them (and to yourself if necessary) that you might try it next year. If it's that great, it will be around next year. If someone is pressuring you to purchase it now or you won't benefit from the service later, run away from it.

The final benefit that I will mention when setting up a budget is that you will be able to track performance versus cost. For example, if you know what you spent on that monthly newsletter and can attribute specific sales to the newsletter, you will be able to figure out if the cost was worth the reward. If you can't attribute many sales to an item, you can ditch that marketing idea going forward and use that money elsewhere.

Be Consistent!

One of the biggest reasons farmers fail is that they give up. They are not consistent at all with their farming. They believe that they should have a listing a week after mailing something to homes. Farming takes time.

I often tell the story of an agent that listed a home in my farm. He did a fair amount of business, just not in my farm. In fact, this was his first listing in the neighborhood that I could recall. He listed the home and immediately sent all of the homes in the neighborhood a beautiful marketing piece. I was intrigued as I was a recipient of that piece, too. I then received a second marketing piece the next week. The third week, something was dropped off at my door. I started to get a little worried. Uh oh. If he kept doing this every week of the year, he would definitely start receiving more listings. However, the other side of my brain was asking how in the world this could be financially beneficial to him. I knew what it cost to do one week's worth of what he did, much less three weeks. Sure enough, he did get another listing a few doors down from the first listing. Good for him. The mailings continued on a weekly basis for eight weeks. One piece was so nice that I kept it in my office until someone asked why I had another agent's marketing material hanging up. I admired it, but I did end up taking it down.

This agent closed both properties, but never received another listing in the farm. After eight weeks, he disappeared. I never received another piece from him. His theory must have been to saturate the market for eight weeks and hope that someone else wanted to list a house. Luckily, someone else did. However, at the end of those two closings and the eight weeks of marketing, do you think he was ahead financially? I would argue probably not. He spent a lot of money to get that second listing. Three months later, if someone needed to list their home, would they remember his name or contact info? How about six months? Nine months?

A year? Odds are good that they would not.

If an agent is visible in the farm on a routine basis, people take notice. They will remember that agent. The marketing material should not only be consistent but look consistent. Your logo should always be on it. If you have a slogan, it should be on it. Your website should be on it. I became known as "Karen", not "Karen Mistrot" because my name on all of my marketing materials was "Karen & Company Realty". If people didn't know my website, they could just search online for Karen and my neighborhood and I would pop up. Or they could ask a neighbor. That happened a lot – someone would talk to someone in the neighborhood and they would say "Call Karen. I have her last newsletter here. I'll send you her contact info." The next thing you know, I am receiving a call from that homeowner.

If I had given up after eight weeks, I wouldn't have been successful in the farm. I persevered and stuck with it. People started to expect to hear from me on a regular basis.

Many agents are taught to send out "Just Listed" and "Just Sold" cards to the surrounding homes of a listing. While that's not a bad idea, if that's all you are doing for the time period that you have the house listed, good luck. You are trying to catch a seller exactly when they need to sell and not a moment later. Don't do it. If it's a home in your farm and you plan on continuing marketing in that neighborhood, then do it.

Be consistent with your marketing. Stick it out. You will see results. It might take six months, but if you are marketing correctly, the business should come to you.

HOA Involvement

This topic may or may not pertain to your situation. In my area of town, HOAs prevailed. It was rare to find a neighborhood without an HOA. As I will discuss in a bit, it's important to not only be aware of the HOA, but also to be involved with them. Anytime I would hold an event in my farm, I let the HOA know about it. I didn't need to get their permission, but I wanted to let them know what I was doing to get their support and to keep my name in front of them on a regular basis. I highly recommend that you do the same if you end up farming a HOA neighborhood.

Direct Mail the Farm Twice a Month for Six Months

By the time you finish this book, you are going to say that I have pounded into your brain the words "Direct Mail Works!". I truly believe it does work. Emails aren't working as people are becoming immune to them. Texts – how much can you really say in a text?

I do think there are ways to successfully farm digitally. Digitally farming can be rewarding. Team it up with direct mail farming and you could have a powerhouse plan on your hands.

If I were just starting to farm a neighborhood, I would try to hit every house twice a month for six months. Basically, I would have the homes receiving something from me every two weeks. After the six months, decide what you want to continue to send out. I mailed out a newsletter eleven months of the year. I also mailed other things periodically, but I knew that at least once a month my farm would receive the newsletter with my information in it.

At the beginning, I would send out a newsletter. More details about that are in the next section. I would also send out market updates. That's what homeowners want to know. What did the house down the street sell for? How long did it take? Be the resource for that information. Coupled with your newsletter, you will be viewed as a true neighborhood expert.

Drive Sellers to Your Website

Always keep in mind that many sellers will look you up on the internet before they call you. Not only do you need a sharp looking website, you need one chock full of information about their neighborhood.

When agents start out in real estate, their companies often provide them with a "free" website. That's great when funds are tight and you are just starting your business. However, you will look like every other agent in your company as everyone has the same type of website. Keep that in mind when you are thinking about creating a new one. Make sure yours is unique. If you are farming, you better have lots of neighborhood information on it, so people know without a doubt that you are the true expert for that area.

Have a strong neighborhood website always helps you with your SEO, or Search Engine Optimization. There are so many resources out there to learn about this subject but be aware that if people are searching for "Happy Valley Ranch Real Estate Agents", you will want your name and website to pop up on that first page. In order for that to happen, you will need a lot of neighborhood content on your site.

Monthly Newsletter

I am a huge believer in a monthly newsletter. I have taken a lot of flak over the years for it, too. Direct mail is dead, no one reads anything in the mail anymore and on and on.

What I can tell you is this. If I was told to get rid of everything in my marketing budget but one item, the newsletter is what I would keep. I would walk into homes and people would have stacks of them on the kitchen table (yes, you can imagine what their house looked like) or they would have the latest one on the kitchen table or hanging on the refrigerator.

Things are very digital right now in the market. I was told numerous times to do an electronic version of the newsletter and I would save so much money and have a bigger impact. This is my theory on that belief. I receive lots of emails each day. I delete those that don't pertain to my life right now as others could be more pressing. It's way too easy to hit "delete". I know that homeowners would do the same thing. Plus, how in the world would I obtain and then maintain thousands of homeowners' email addresses? People change them like they change their clothes. They have secret emails that they stick their "junk email" into. I didn't want to get buried. One thing that didn't change in my farm was the physical addresses of homes.

When I began in real estate almost one hundred percent of my business came from my newsletter. Years later, it was still the basis for my farming. Why was it so successful? Was it just a gorgeous piece of material? I wish!

As I stated early on, when I started farming, I wasn't sure

what I was doing and definitely didn't know it was called "farming". I started a newsletter and used the old Microsoft Publisher program to create it. I just used one of the pre-defined templates. Boy, if I had known that I would be creating that newsletter every month for over fourteen years, I may have put some more thought into it. Why? Well, once people began to expect the newsletter to look a certain way in their mailboxes, I couldn't change it. I had to keep the same color paper, the same format, etc. If I changed it, I risked people not recognizing it and throwing it away. My pro tip here – put a lot of thought into what your newsletter looks like as you may use it for many years.

What's the secret sauce to get people to read the newsletters? This is by far the biggest tip for the newsletter. Don't use a canned newsletter. I repeat, do not use a canned newsletter. There are many companies out there that will solicit you and suggest that they can send out a newsletter for you and all you need to do is provide your logo, your contact info and the magic credit card. Boy, other than having to pay for it by credit card, that sounds so tempting to agents. I admit, some months I wished I had bought a service such as this.

Unfortunately, there are several problems with canned newsletters. One, they can typically add up price-wise. Two, they will always look "fake". Sure, you can add some personal touches to the newsletter, but it will still look "canned". I lived in Colorado and I received a "canned" newsletter from an agent. One of the top articles one month was about caring for your palm trees. I never owned or even saw a palm tree in Colorado. It immediately struck me as "fake". Consumers aren't dumb. They will know it's canned information and throw it away every month. They won't give you another chance. They will just assume that it's not useful information.

The third problem with canned newsletters is that you typically don't know the exact date that one will be delivered. I am very sensitive about this because I made a lot of mistakes. If my newsletter was delivered on a Friday or Saturday, I heard crickets. Nothing. Nada. If it was delivered during a holiday week such as Thanksgiving, same thing. Nothing. Spring Break for the kids? I might as well have just put that money into a slot machine. I wasn't going to hear anything from anyone. I learned that in my market the newsletter needed to hit the mailboxes on Wednesdays or Thursdays. In our farm, people were receiving bulk coupons in the mail on Tuesdays and my newsletter was easily mixed into the coupons and could be thrown into the trash. To get the most bang for my buck, I needed it to be delivered on

Wednesdays or Thursdays. I learned that if I dropped off the newsletter at our Bulk Mail Department (which is in a Post Office) on a Tuesday, it would be in my farms' mailboxes on Wednesday. If I paid a service to mail out the newsletter, I would lose control of that delivery date. It would be an estimate. I couldn't risk it. Too much money and business were at stake.

A fourth problem with the canned newsletter idea is that I would never really know if they caught on that there was one street that should get that newsletter because they were in the farm or if they were just using a mile radius address list. I wanted control of who received the newsletter and that could actually change month to month for me.

The final and biggest problem was the content. As I said, canned newsletters tend to be, well, canned. I needed to provide hyper-local content that homeowners wanted to know about. The key for me was creating a newsletter with local information in it. I had one section that was my bread and butter. It was called "What is Being Built Where...". People loved it. I am not exaggerating when I say that I received many, many emails and calls from people just thanking me for sending out the newsletter. They would tell me that they obtained more information from my newsletter than anywhere else.

My theory with that section was born out of my own frustration. How many times do you drive by a building in your own neighborhood and notice something being built but there is no sign telling you, the consumer, what they are doing? I am always shocked by that fact. What a waste of a marketing opportunity by the business! How about a restaurant that closed? Do people wonder what happened? I would go to social gatherings in my neighborhood and what would everyone talk about? Local happenings. They wanted to know what was being built in a building. They wanted to know why a restaurant closed and if something else was going into that spot.

My newsletter became that resource. Yes, it took time to research and write that section every month, but it was read every single month. As time went by, businesses contacted me directly to tell me about what going on with their business. Residents would call and text me with information, too!

I had a system down to get this information for the newsletter. You may have a better idea of how to get the info and if so, go for it. I just would drive around my farm with intention. Sure, I drove around a lot as it was and noticed things. On newsletter creation days, I really drove around. I would pull over and run up to contractors and ask what they were building. I would talk to neighboring businesses to find out what they knew. I would read permits on the door. I would also just jot tips down in my phone, so I would remember to research something later. I could find a lot of information online through the businesses websites, the city's website or the county's website, but nothing beat talking to people in person. It actually became pretty easy to find things to write about.

When the economy was not so hot, it almost became a "What is Closing Around Town" column. It was challenging to put a positive spin on things, but I did it. One thing I will mention is that you might hear negative things about a business. Perhaps theories as to why a business closed. I never, ever wrote about that. I would say that the business had closed, but the reader had to figure out why. Unless a business was moving to a new location, I never second-guessed a closing. I also was very, very careful to post only confirmed closings. Many of these businesses were Mom and Pop businesses. I didn't want to hurt their business.

I often would try to write the column with some humor. One month I wrote about a Jack in the Box fast food franchise opening in our town. It was the first one. My husband truly loved Jack in the Box and was beside himself with excitement. He couldn't wait to buy their tacos. I happened to put that in my newsletter and said that we would probably be the first ones in town to be there when they opened. I can't tell you how many people asked me about it. They wanted to make sure my husband ordered his tacos! Years later, one of the restaurants closed. My husband had talked me into going with him to lunch there, but we didn't know it was closed. It had actually just happened and quite suddenly, too. My husband had the saddest face sitting in that parking lot. I took a quick photo on my phone and posted it on social media. People were sending us condolences! People loved learning a little bit more about me – it made the column much more personal.

What else did I put in the newsletter? I typically always had a section detailing the neighborhood real estate statistics. How many homes were on the market, how many were under contract and how many had sold year to date. I included average prices and days on the market. I was a real estate agent after all – I needed to know those stats on a regular basis.

The back page of my newsletter just listed my inventory. I would show current listings, my under-contract listings and my solds. Think about it. You could get at least three months of print time with one listing. One month when it's listed, another month when it's under contract and the third month when it's sold. If it was a slow month and I didn't have much to show, I always had something else to fill in that section. Maybe I was doing a neighborhood event – what a perfect place to advertise it!

Over the years, I toyed around with the idea of printing it in color, of making it a larger newsletter and also putting ads in the newsletter. I ended up not doing any of them. Why? Again, people expected it to look a certain way. Printing it in color would look nice, but my cost per newsletter would have increased dramatically. Finally, getting advertisers in the newsletter was tempting. I could have it funded simply with ads. I didn't do that for a few reasons. One, I really didn't have the space – I used every inch of my newsletter. Two, I didn't want to get into the business of determining advertisement costs and then worry about collecting it, etc. Finally, I realized that readers might make some assumptions about me with certain advertisers. Let's say that I let a national bank with a local branch advertise in the newsletter. Well, I know for a fact that someone out there would have had a bad experience with the national bank. Who knows what the problem really was, but they could see my ad and assume that I only worked with that bank and decide that they didn't want to work with me based on that fact alone. I worked too hard to establish my brand and reputation to have it eliminated in a second based on an advertisement.

How did I determine how to mail it? I used mailing route codes and therefore could utilize the "bulk mail" lower mailing rate. You can easily find out what route codes are in your farm online. The United States Postal Service has a great resource online to determine the route codes for every street out there. I knew all of my routing codes and simply sent the newsletter to my local printer and told him the route codes I needed. He printed the newsletter off and sorted them into the route codes for me. I picked up the newsletters and dropped them off at our local Bulk Mail Department in the post office. I'm sure that other printers would do all of that for you, but it might cost a bit more. I also needed a Bulk Mail Permit that was placed on each newsletter. My printer had one and just put it on the newsletter.

The nice thing about doing it this way was that I knew exactly when the newsletters would be delivered. At my post office, if I dropped them off one day, almost all of the newsletters would be delivered the next day. I could control my delivery date by bringing them to the post office myself.

I do want to mention that you don't even have to mail the newsletter. If your farm size isn't too big, you could drop the newsletters off at each door. It will really teach you more about the neighborhood as you walk around. Just be aware of any non-solicitation rules that might be in effect with the neighborhood. You may end up chatting with some homeowners at the same time as you save some money!

HOA Newsletters

If your farm has a HOA newsletter, advertise in it. You need to be seen everywhere associated with the neighborhood. Sometimes, the advertising fee can be minimal, especially for a business card size ad.

Speaking of business card size ads, don't just send in your business card. That really does nothing for you. I obtained several listing appointments because people thought that the business card ad agent did no business in the neighborhood. How did they get that impression? The agent's office address was listed on their card. Many times, agents' offices are not in their farm area. Not a big deal to the agent, but it can send out the wrong signal to the sellers. They want someone in their neighborhood.

If you are going to pay for any sized ad, make it worth your while. A business card does not tell a seller why they should call you. It just says that you are an agent. Maybe you live in the neighborhood. That's a big deal. Make sure your ad says something like "It's not just my business, it's my neighborhood, too". Tell them you have lived in the area for "X" number of years, basically give them a reason to call you based on your expertise, not based on your photo, phone number or office address.

Another tip that I would pass on with HOA ads is to see if you can negotiate a long-term price for the ad. I wanted the back page of my newsletter. I figured that I had at minimum a 50/50 shot at being seen. Once when the homeowner removed it from their mailbox and another time when they put it in the trash. At the time, the HOA needed the advertising money. I was able to negotiate a multi-year deal for a very reasonable amount. Once the time period was up, they played hardball with me because another agent had been inquiring about that space. He was determined to get the ad location. I had to pony up more money just to keep my space. I probably should have negotiated for a longer time period.

I also advertised in email versions of HOA newsletters in other farms. After trying them out for over a year and getting absolutely nothing in return, I stopped advertising in the electronic newsletter versions. Many residents didn't even know that they could sign up for the newsletters, had changed their email address and didn't tell the HOA or just deleted the email. The advertising rates were super-cheap, but I received nothing in return.

Advertise in the farm when you know homeowners will be receiving the ads.

Volunteer to Write a Home Helper Column – Free!

Many times, HOA newsletters are looking for content. They need something to fill up the newsletter. I asked several times before the HOA newsletter let me submit a monthly column. I volunteered to send in several columns at a time so they didn't have to worry. The content was easy for me. I just asked a common question that I received and provided a response. For example, what can I do to increase my home's curb appeal? Should I remodel and stay or just buy a new home? What are the top three things I can do to increase my home's value right now? You get the drift. Stuff that most agents answer on a regular basis. I wrote the columns and of course, put a plug at the end of the column about my company and how we lived in the neighborhood, etc. etc.

Attend HOA Meetings – Free!

I know, I know. You would rather get a root canal than go to a HOA meeting. I get it. However, you can find out tons of information in these meetings. Plus, you get to know the

HOA board members. You may very well need their help down the road, so it doesn't hurt to let them know who you are.

I attended HOA meetings for different reasons. I always introduced myself and said that I might not live in the neighborhood, but I was hoping to do more business in it, so I wanted to learn as much as possible. I was never turned away. Instead, I was greeted with surprise that an agent would take the time to come to a meeting or with a snarky comment like "It's about time that an agent tried to learn something before they sold a house in this neighborhood,". Sometimes the HOA board would have to go into "executive sessions" and I couldn't stay for those, but that was okay.

Other than learning more information about a farm, why should you go to HOA meetings? They increase your credibility a great deal. For instance, I was at more than one listing appointment where a house down the street was often discussed. The homeowners always wanted to know if "that" house would ruin their chances for a sale. The house had been painted a pretty hideous shade of peach. Peach might work in some communities. In that neighborhood, it stood out like a sore thumb. However, I had actually been at the meeting where that color had been approved! In the HOA board members' defense, I have to say that the color looked quite different on paper than on the house. When I told neighbors about the approval, they were stunned but at the same time they were impressed that I knew so much about it. Did it win me listings? You bet it did.

Start a Neighborhood Directory – Low Cost!

When I talk about starting a neighborhood directory, I often get met with a lot of resistance from agents. They will say that no one will participate, that confidentiality is at risk, you name it. Here's what I can tell you. The neighborhood directories were a hit in my neighborhood. I didn't do them for thousands of people. I just handpicked my own little section of homes. Since I was farming, I was involved in the neighborhood. People started to know who I was and that I lived in the neighborhood.

Initially, I sent out postcards and asked people to participate. I made sure that they knew that the information would not be provided to anyone else for marketing purposes. I asked people to email me specific information. It did take a couple of years to get almost everyone on board. People might have been skeptical as to what I was going to do with the information, but when they realized that I was not going to sell the info or spam them, they were good with it.

I asked for their names, addresses, kids' names and dates of birth, schools that the kids attended, phone numbers and then any miscellaneous information that they wanted to provide. There really was a method to my madness. I wanted the kids' dates of births because I didn't want to keep changing kids' ages. People are sensitive about that stuff – maybe Tommy turned six years old two weeks before I dropped off the directory. I didn't want to deal with that problem. I also asked for schools because in my neighborhood, kids could opt to go to a variety of schools. Parents often didn't realize that someone else two streets over had kids in the same school. I asked for miscellaneous information for babysitters, pet sitters, home business information. People loved that I included this information and my directory became a resource for all of those things.

I never included email addresses, even though many neighbors asked me to do so. When I explained why I didn't do it, they quickly agreed. Basically, if I provided email addresses, I ran the risk of a neighbor spamming their own neighbors to tell them about their businesses or just their own frustrations with the neighborhood (think "picking up dog poop", "cars parked overnight on the street"). They could be well-intended, but it was a quick way for someone to say that they didn't want their information included in my directory. No one wants to receive spam email, so I didn't include that information.

I would update the directory on an annual basis. I did it at the beginning of the year as that is when people start thinking about selling in the Spring. I wanted my name out there. I mailed postcards and I also posted signs at the entries and exits to the neighborhood reminding people to send me their updated information by February 1. I included my email address on the signs.

I also wanted those email addresses. I had basically created a neighborhood email list that I closely coveted. I will tell you more about it in just a bit, but I emailed those neighbors to remind them about the directory as well. Many times, neighbors would tell other neighbors to get into my directory.

Other agents often recommended that I put the directory online. I attempted to do that one year and was met with resistance from the neighbors. They said that they wanted a resource in their house that they could just go grab. Sure enough, I often saw that directory on a desk or counter when I went into listing appointments.

Volunteer at Local Schools/Organizations – Free!

If you have children in a school in your farm, this could be super easy to do. Schools always need volunteers. Maybe parents are needed for organizing a school's talent show, parents for lunch duty, parents for the Parent Teacher Organizations and the list goes on.

If you don't have children in the school, think about how else you could volunteer. I had a gentleman in one of my farming classes say, "Won't the school think it's creepy if I want to volunteer at a school and I don't even have kids?". Yes, they could. However, it's all in how you present yourself. Talk to the school's front desk. Tell them that you are a real estate agent that does a lot of business in the school's neighborhood and you want to give back. Ask how you can help. In another farming class that I taught, a gentleman spoke up and said that he plays the guitar and volunteered at a local school to sing silly songs to kindergarteners while he plays the guitar. He has a standing Friday invitation.

You could do the same thing with local organizations such as the Rotary Club, Chamber of Commerce, MOPS (Mothers of Preschoolers), local animal shelters, etc.

A couple words of warning at this point. One, volunteer doing something that you enjoy. Don't dread volunteering.

Your lack of enthusiasm will become apparent very quickly and you may find reasons why you just can't volunteer that week. Two, don't go into the volunteering gig with the thought that you must get business out of it. It will happen over time if you are authentic with your volunteering time. If you meet someone on the first day volunteering and start to tell them that you are a real estate agent and then ask if they need any real estate assistance, wow. You just turned them off and they will probably avoid you at all costs. On the other hand, if you volunteer and get to know other people, the natural conversations will direct themselves to what you do for a living, how do you like it, etc. You will want to ask those questions of others in the group, too. Don't forget – you are there to help with the organization first and foremost. After that, you could become a valuable asset to that organization and your name will come to mind if someone has a real estate need.

Create a Neighborhood Watch Program – Free!

I know that every area is different, but in my County and many others, the Neighborhood Watch programs are free to implement. The Programs just need someone to take charge of them!

I happened to farm a neighborhood that had a

Neighborhood Watch program already implemented. Unfortunately (or fortunately in my case), it only encompassed half of the entire neighborhood. The other half were newer homes and the person in charge of the program kind of ignored that portion. I called the local Sheriff's office (yours may be the local police department) and talked to them about starting the program for the other side of the neighborhood. Today, all of this information is now online, and instructions are very easy.

I sent out emails and postcards to people (and put it in my monthly newsletter) to see if anyone wanted to participate. I had a great response. Yes, people wanted to be involved. Who doesn't want to know how to remain safe in their home? Plus, they wanted to know if crimes were occurring around the area. By being the coordinator, I started to receive updates on the local crimes and in turn would send out emails to the neighbors about the crimes happening. Luckily, there were not many, but everyone wanted to know about them. Homeowners wanted to be on that email list. I became the resource for the neighborhood. Someone's home was broken into in my neighborhood. I ended up talking to the homeowner right after the police were called. He wanted me to make sure to get the word out to see if anyone knew anything or had seen it happen.

Overall, it was an inexpensive way for me to meet people and at the same time become a go-to resource for the farm.

Create a Neighborhood Email List – Free!

As you can see, I was emailing information to people pretty often. I started off with a small list of emails, but it quickly grew. I had people contacting me asking to be added to the list often.

The key ingredient to this list being valuable to homeowners was that I never marketed to them. What? Why else would I want to take the time to send out emails? Well, I wanted to be that resource for them. My email signature always said what I did for a living, how I sold the most homes in the farm, etc. I didn't need to pound the email recipient over the head that with information. I never once sent out an email to the farm saying that they should check out my latest listing or that they should call me to list their home.

Instead, I sent out valuable information to them. What crimes had happened was much more valuable to them than me asking them to look at a house I just listed. I became the person that was told when a pet was lost. People would email me a picture of the pet and ask me to send out an email to everyone. I can't tell you how many "lost pet emails" I sent out in my day. However, people remembered me. I would send out information about local businesses that were being built right next to the farm, so homeowners would know if they would be impacted.

I did have requests from other people to just share the email list with them. I never did. It was too valuable and had taken me time and effort to obtain the information. Plus, people wanted the list, so they could sell something to the email recipient. That went against what I used the list for and I knew that people would start asking to be removed from the list. The entire time I used my list I never had anyone ask to be removed unless they had moved away from the area.

Create a Neighborhood Networking Group

Okay, I have to be honest with this one. I did this for several years and I did get business from doing it. However, I eventually disbanded it because it was one big headache. I still think it's a great idea, but I would implement this in a very different fashion today. Learn from my mistakes!

I started a Neighborhood Networking Group. I thought it would be a great idea to share leads with each other. You know, a realtor sharing leads with a roofing company that happened to be owned by someone in the farm. A plumber that was also looking for business. Basically, it was going to be a leads group, but all of us would be living in the same neighborhood.

I started the group by advertising it in my monthly newsletter. I received lots of interest. I set up the meetings in our neighborhood clubhouse. I brought snacks for the meeting and put the meeting agenda together. After all, I wanted the meetings to be productive and not just a "stand around and eat" kind of thing.

As I mentioned, I did get business out of this group. People still talk about it to this day and I haven't run it in years. Unfortunately, it could have run more smoothly and would have been more productive if I had just done a few things differently.

First, I paid for that clubhouse every month. I shouldn't have done that. I should have implemented some type of fee to be in the group to cover expenses or I should have just said that meetings would be held at a local restaurant's meeting room where everyone would be expected to buy breakfast, lunch, etc. to cover the cost of the room. I also provided the snacks. No one else would volunteer so I thought that I should do it. Another mistake I made was that I created the agenda. Maybe I should have done that for six months and then turned it over to another person to handle for six months and on and on. It became a chore for me to handle. My last mistake was that I didn't publish any membership guidelines. I was learning as I went along. People were joining to promote their multi-level marketing business and were trying to recruit other members to be on their "teams". That type of solicitation totally turned off members who in turn asked me to get the multi-level marketers out of the group. I also had numerous people want to join from one profession. For instance, several roofing companies wanted to join. Did we really need five roofers? Nope. Just one.

If I did this today, I would set up rules and expectations from the get-go. I might also charge a fee to be in the group, so we could see who was serious. I would also not put myself on the hook financially for the meeting space and food.

If you take these comments and apply them to your own group, I think you could have a very successful, productive Neighborhood Networking Group!

Host "How to Get Your Home SOLD!" Sessions

This very successful idea worked really well in my farm. I would advertise a "How to Get Your Home SOLD!" session and hold it somewhere in the farm – the community center, a school, etc. I held this event in a variety of markets. When the market was tough, I talked about how to get their home sold. When it was a robust market and people were worried that they would be homeless because their home would sell too quickly, I talked about their options.

Here's what I did: I advertised the session in my newsletter, on social media and sometimes postcards. The session would be about an hour long during the week. I started doing them in the "hot" thinking-about-listing months of January, February and March. I held them at least once a month. I simply put together a Power Point presentation and displayed it on a tv in the room I rented. Super simple as my agenda consisted of telling people who I was, what the market was truly doing (myth versus reality), what sellers really needed to do to get their home sold (necessary repairs), the importance of staging and professional photography and at the end, questions that they needed to ask a real estate agent when they interviewed them.

Over the years of doing real estate, I realized that people really had misconceptions of what they should do to their home to prepare it to sell. Some sellers thought that they didn't have to do a thing in a hot market while others thought that they needed to completely remodel their kitchen or bathroom. Some thought that they shouldn't clean that dirty carpet until the house sold. All of these perceptions were incorrect. The list goes on. I simply talked about what was important in my farm. For instance, for a very long time my farm houses had wood shake roofs. They were really "in" at the time the neighborhood was built. However, as time went by, the roofs became damaged and if not maintained, they looked really bad. Insurance on these roofs was also higher than normal. The HOA also didn't allow anyone to replace their wood shake roof with another wood shake roof. They were just not the thing buyers wanted.

I can't tell you how many sellers told me that I should just tell the buyers to wait until the next hail storm and then they could get it covered by insurance. Hmmm.... I would always say "How has that concept worked for you?". That would just shut that idea down. They had lived in their home for 15 years and apparently a hail storm had not occurred yet. I strongly recommended that the homeowners obtain roof certifications for their roofs. I won't go into detail on these, but if you haven't heard about them, they basically provide a buyer without a little bit more coverage if something happens to the roof.

Most sellers had never even heard of the roof certifications and quickly started getting them after our session. Did I give away "free advice"? Perhaps. However, it only helped my farm in the long run.

As far as being "homeless", in Colorado we had a "Post Occupancy Agreement" at the time. Basically, it was a form that allowed sellers to stay in their home for a short period of time after they sold the house. Agents knew about it. I quickly learned that the general public did not know about it. Once I described this as a potential opportunity for them to have more time to find their next home, it was like a huge weight was lifted off of their shoulders. They were then ready to list their home because they would have that cushion of time to find their next home.

I loved doing these sessions because I also had an opportunity to sell myself. Homeowners could tell that I knew the neighborhood. When I reviewed staging and professional photography, they learned that I implemented both of these things in my business automatically. Many of my competitors would not provide staging or professional photos and it showed – houses sold for less and in a longer time period. As I went through questions that they might ask real estate agents, two things happened. One, an "ah ha" moment occurred with many sellers. They thought that all agents were the same and maybe they should just go with their cousin, co-worker, etc. They quickly realized that we all weren't the same. Two, I answered the questions for myself as I went through the answers and they learned a lot about how I did business. I was able to sell myself and my services during the event.

I was never a "hard sell" during these events. I kept the sessions as "information gathering" meetings. At the end of the meeting, I suggested that if they wanted an idea of what their home was worth today and what they might need to do to get it ready to sell, I would be happy to set up a time to come over. I always, always obtained listings using this event.

Many agents have asked how many people really attended these sessions. I didn't have a Standing Room Only situation. I always had about 10-15 attendees. This may not sound like much, but guess what? Those 10-15 people were very serious about selling their homes and doing it relatively quickly. I would have conducted those meetings every night of the week if I could get in front of 10-15 serious home sellers in my farm every time. The smaller size also allowed for a lot of questions which helped everyone.

As the years went by, I stopped doing them. To be honest, I had no idea why I stopped. I finally asked myself one November why I had stopped. No reason. I thought that I should start them up again, but this time I would offer up webinars! After all, I loved taking classes via a webinar. They were so easy, and I could take them from the comfort of my office or home. I didn't have to worry if a snowstorm might create a traffic nightmare. I signed up for a webinar service. Created the webinar and started to advertise. I thought that I could do a lot more of them since I was simply doing them from my computer.

That idea suffered a very quick death. I learned that my farm did not want a webinar. Instead, they still wanted an old-fashioned in-person meeting. It didn't matter if it was sunny or snowing. People showed up. Your farm demographic might differ, and a webinar might work. Just be open to doing this event in different ways.

Donate to Schools or Advertise in Their Materials

Another way to become the "go-to" agent in a neighborhood is to donate to local schools or advertise with them. If the parents keep seeing your information everywhere, you quickly become the expert real estate agent. However, I do have a word of caution. Always make sure that you are the only real estate agent advertising. I learned this the hard way. Typically, the school donation coordinators are parents and they change every year as their own kids get older. Most of these folks won't understand the importance of you being the only real estate agent advertising. Your message gets diluted if you are one of three agents advertising on the same banner or at the same event. Yes, you may end up paying a little bit more for that privilege, but you will also become known as the "go-to" person when the school needs something. Just simply explain the importance of being the only agent and they will "get it".

I can still walk into schools and people at the front desk will know who I am and start talking real estate. Do you think that the real estate topic comes up often in schools? You bet it does. Who will they think of when talking to someone about selling their home or buying in the neighborhood? I wanted it to be me.

I mentioned that I learned this the hard way. I was approached about six to eight months before a "fun run" event at an elementary school about donating to the event. I immediately said yes. I didn't put any parameters around it. I donated quite a bit. When the event was about to happen, I started to see some videos on social media about it, but never noticed my name being advertised. I drove over to the school and saw a big banner on the corner. I wasn't even on it. However, another agent sure was prominently listed. It ends up that he paid a premium to get on that banner, unbeknownst to me. Sure, it would have been smart for the school to contact me and ask if I would want to do something similar to be prominently displayed on t-shirts or something like that, but they didn't. Again, these are parent volunteers, not necessarily business people trying to maximize exposure. My donation went down the drown. I was on some material, but basically my information was buried.

Donate to Local Sports Teams

If your farm has a local sports team, donate to it. Don't just think about donating money. Many times, these teams need other items.

For instance, for the local high school football/baseball/basketball team, why not donate water bottles with a customized label on them? Just buy some water bottle blank labels (yes, there are such things) and make your own label with your information on it. Wrap the labels around the water bottles and then donate them to the sports teams. They can sell them and make a profit and your name gets out there.

I have found that donating items rather than just money has a bigger impact. People remember you as they are walking around with the water bottle.

You could also have a banner at the sports field.

Sometimes this can cost some money, so be careful. I ended up paying to put up a banner on a fence siding to a high school. It wasn't for a specific sport, but every day people drove by the school (which was in my farm) and saw my sign.

I also donated to our local swim team every year. This swim team was very popular and many, many kids were on it. The parents had to agree to volunteer for their kids to be allowed on the team. After a few years of being buried with other agents, I struck a deal with the swim team. I would donate money and in return be the only agent on a t-shirt and in a program. I also had a banner hung and they would announce me at the meets as a sponsor. What really ended up helping was when I thought out of the box. The swim team had a very strong parent volunteer base and was very organized. I volunteered to donate coffee, creamer, sugar, stir sticks and cups for their concession stand. The concessions were a big money maker for the team. In return for my donation, they hung my banner over the concession stand. I also found a company that made coffee cup sleeves. I was able to get my logo printed on the sleeves. When people bought the coffee, one of my sleeves went on the outside.

Parents and other adults (grandparents, aunts, uncles) would then walk around the swim meets with my name on their coffee cup. I was targeting them as the kids didn't buy or sell houses. I know this worked because I listed several houses due to my sponsorship of the swim team. Sellers told me that was important to them. I also would receive texts and emails from people holding up those coffee cups saying, "Hey Karen, guess what I just bought?".

If I had just donated money, I wouldn't have received at least half of the same exposure. Thinking "out of the box" really helped me create more awareness of my brand in my farm.

Attend Local Events, Be Seen in the Farm – Free!

If you are farming a neighborhood, you will want to know as much information about it as possible. How can you find out this info? By attending meetings. You'll find that some of these meetings are not well-attended which is a sad, but realistic situation. However, you will stand out at the meeting as someone who did take the time to come. You can find out a ton of information just by going to the meetings.

At some meetings – let's say there is a meeting about changing trash providers – you may see a lot of people in attendance. Guess what? They will see you there, too. I was told often that someone saw me at a meeting. Then they would ask my opinion about the topic of the meeting. Word got out that I was involved in the farm. Free publicity for my business and my brand.

Create Neighborhood Videos

An easy and fun idea is to create neighborhood videos. If you have talent in the video arena, you might want to create them yourself. It's pretty easy to do these days just with your phone and some video software. You don't need to purchase expensive software either. Apple's iMovie is terrific and is free. On the Windows front, try the free MovieMaker. Of course, if you want to have a few more video tricks up your sleeve, invest in some software on your own. The last option is to hire someone to create the videos for you. Many times, you can find high school or even college students that will do it for a very reasonable amount, sometimes just dinner will do the trick!

What do you include in the videos? Yourself, but just at the beginning, possibly for a couple of seconds in the middle and then again at the end. You can also do the voiceover as the video is showing the viewer a neighborhood. Highlight what makes your farm so unique. Does it have terrific amenities? Perhaps it is in a great location? Schools in the area? You get the idea.

The video should really be under three minutes or you will lose viewers. No one wants to watch a ten-minute video about a neighborhood. Why does the creation of such a neighborhood video help you? Well, you will post that baby just about everywhere that you can. Definitely have it on your website. When people are searching for that neighborhood online, your video should pop up early in the search bracket unless there are lots of others out there. At the time of this writing, search engines absolutely love videos and will give them more credit. In addition, your website showcasing the neighborhood with your video will provide another reason for the viewer to believe that you must be the neighborhood expert. Post it on your social media. You'll be surprised at how many views you will receive. Make sure you have it on your YouTube channel (yes, you should have one of those, but don't worry they are pretty easy to create). I even posted it in my local MLS for my farm listings as a supplemental video to the house video. It made a difference to buyers. They might love the way a house looks online, but then when they see the neighborhood, it really cinches the deal for them. They want to see the house and this terrific neighborhood!

Chapter 8

Many More Farming Examples

When you start farming, you will want even more ideas of things that you might want to do. I was always searching for creative and new ideas. I am about to throw a ton of them at you. When I teach this class, I inevitably get asked "Do you ever sleep?". You have to keep in mind as you go through this section that I did not do every one of these ideas every single year. I just couldn't do that financially or even professionally. If I did so, I would have gone broke and I would have been known as that ever-so-annoying agent that just advertises and never sells houses.

The forthcoming examples may not have been stellar successes in a few cases, but I will be brutally honest and tell you why I think that happened. If they are included in this section, they have strong potential. I didn't include any "duds"! So, let's get started.

Food Truck Frenzy

I typically liked to do one big farm event a year. You may not be able to do that yourself, especially when you are starting out. However, keep in mind the idea of partnering with someone. Perhaps a lender, inspector, etc. At one of my classes, I explained how the Food Truck Frenzy worked for me and a lender approached me after the class. She said she would be happy to go in half with me the next time I offered it.

With any event, you will want to start the planning sooner rather than later. The Food Truck Frenzy was no exception. I started planning it about four to five months prior to the event. In Colorado, weather is always a factor for events. I didn't want to run the risk of a snowstorm cancelling this event, so I decided to hold it as late as I was comfortable with in the Fall. I would have preferred to hold it in early September, but I needed a location in the farm. The best location was near our neighborhood pools. The pools weren't closing until mid-September, so I waited until the end of that month to hold the event.

Here's how it worked. I was not a food truck connoisseur. True confession. I had never bought a single thing from a food truck. However, I knew people were in love with them. So I started reaching out to people to see if they had any favorite trucks. I then started online research. It's funny when you become focused on something how it starts appearing before you all of the time. Once I decided to host this event, I started seeing food trucks everywhere. I would jot down their info. I also would try to check them out. For example, my husband and I stopped at a local car show just to see how the whole food truck thing worked and which ones were popular.

I started calling the trucks and tried to get them to agree to come to the event. No small feat since I had no idea how many people would actually show up. However, I did know that in the past, the neighborhood Fall Festivals were well attended. The HOA was not hosting those any longer so this event's timing was perfect. I estimated that 300 people might be there. That attracted some food truck attention.

I also realized that I needed some other ambience, so I hired a local DJ (every event is better with music), a balloon artist and a spray tattoo artist. I set up a cornhole game, bought some cheap frisbees and put my logo on them (just stickers) and rented some table and chairs. I ordered some re-usable signs to put around the neighborhood on the Thursday before the Saturday event. I also ordered a banner in order that I could install it around the event and people would remember who was hosting the thing.

Although I had a tent and table with our banner on it, I decided that I wanted to give away something so people would come talk to me. I bought a lot of water bottles on sale. White labeled bottles are the best. I then bought some blank Avery water bottle labels and put my logo on the labels. I wrapped the labels around the water bottles and handed them out. People would walk around with my logo everywhere. So many people just came up to talk to us to thank us for hosting the event.

Our biggest problem was the food truck world itself. Little did I know that it would be murder to get most of these truck owners to confirm. I was holding my breath that they would show up and that was after numerous phone calls. Sure enough, one didn't show up at all and one showed up midway through the event. All but one of the trucks ran out of food which was very unusual for them. Needless to say, all of them were very enthusiastic about the event and wanted to be invited back for the next one.

When it was all said and done, we had almost 600 people attend the event over a three-hour period. It was a huge success. Did we sell houses during the event? No. However, we talked a lot of real estate. We also were thanked a ton for not only doing the event, but for supporting the neighborhood throughout the year and for our newsletter. Yes, that newsletter did receive lots of praise.

I also realized that I wanted to get my bang for my buck with this event. I decided to hold a raffle for a Target gift card if attendees would participate in a short video about the neighborhood. Basically, I gave them a microphone and we recorded them telling us why they loved living in the neighborhood. People said that no one would do it. They were wrong. People willingly lined up to be in the video. Maybe it was the Target gift card. Who knows? I knew a lot about the neighborhood, but to hear these people gush about it on video really did get to me. I had each person sign a release saying that I could use the video for future advertising. We edited the videos together (on iMovie) and created a short video about why people liked living in the neighborhood. Of course, I posted it everywhere afterwards and emailed it to the participants. Guess who shared that video? Yep. The participants. I was able to get even more mileage out of that video. I started to put it as a supplemental video in my farm listings, too. Very powerful information as the message was coming from current residents of the farm!

Finally, we did a quick summary video of the event. I posted that on social media as well and said something like "Look what you missed if you didn't make it to the Food Truck Frenzy"! Again, lots of goodwill occurred just from that video.

While this event did take some time and some money, it was well worth it. I could have had other sponsors there, too.

I just chose not to do so. We were the sole sponsor, so we really did get attention.

"Yappy" Halloween!

Another event that is a little "out there" is a "Yappy" Halloween Costume Contest and Parade. Full disclosure. I saw this idea being done in another neighborhood in Houston. The neighborhood was much smaller than my farm, but I saw pictures and could tell how much the residents loved it! I decided that I would try to do it on a larger scale.

Basically, I set up a Saturday morning before Halloween as "Yappy" Halloween day. Residents of the farm could enter their dogs into the costume contest and then have them trot their way down a parade path in the neighborhood. My biggest risk with this event was of course the Colorado weather. By the end of October, I was taking a huge risk. In Colorado, the big storms seemed to arrive later in the day, so I wanted to do this event in the morning.

I went to local vendors and asked if they would like to be judges and perhaps contribute something towards a gift bag for the winners. I had a vet, pet sitters, dog trainers and more volunteer. I allowed them to have a booth free of charge at the event. I also contacted the local high school (which was right across the street from this event) and talked to the National Honor Society sponsor. It ends up that the National Honor Society kids had to complete community service hours every year. I asked if my event could be included for consideration. Sure enough, it was. I had six teenage volunteers immediately. Yahoo!

Residents were directed to my website (great for SEO purposes!) to sign up their pet. If they had more than one dog, they might be entered into the "Duo" or "Group" category. After all, "Sonny and Cher" kind of had an advantage over a sole dog dressed up as a clown.

We had donuts available for people to munch on as they roamed around. We asked people to check in thirty minutes before the contest started. The teenage volunteers checked them in. They signed a release saying we could video them and their dogs for advertising purposes. After they checked in, they were provided a number on an eight and a half by eleven piece of paper. I insisted that all dogs were on a leash, by the way. I didn't want any dog fights to be happening!

When the contest started, another teenage volunteer routed the contestants up to the stage in number order. Yes, I rented a stage and short stairs (we are talking dogs that had to go up the stairs so they had to be short). The judges were at a table in the front. I announced the dog and its costume to the crowd. "Here's Max in his super-cool Batman costume!". The owner had to hold up the piece of paper with a number on it, so the judges could just remember the number and not the name of the dog. After all, we might have had a couple of "Spot's" entered and we didn't want to mix them up.

After they trotted across the stage (to music such as "Who Let the Dogs Out"), another teenage volunteer directed them to the parade path. We had another couple of teenage volunteers directing traffic along the parade route. Other residents set up chairs along the path to watch the Pooch Parade! The parade was routed back to the main stage area. By then, we had the results and announced the winners.

Overall, it was a quick event, but totally fun and very engaging. I created a marketing piece to hand out at the event to attendees stating "Thinking Fido needs a new home – bigger, smaller or just maybe more yard for him to roam? Give Karen & Company a call to provide a complimentary market analysis of your home! You might be surprised!". Yes, they might be surprised. Our market at the time was doing well so there was always that factor. But of course, you always have those sellers who think their home is worth double what the market dictates, so they might be surprised with my analysis, too!

Of course, we did the summary video at the end and emailed it to all of the contestants' owners. We published it everywhere. Lots of good will and great exposure for us!

Host a Back to School/End of School Party

These are pretty easy to create and are usually well-attended. You can easily find out what date school is out in the area. If you have more than one date for various schools, I would use the elementary school dates for this event. If you have more than one elementary school in the area and they each end on different dates, go with the last date.

Basically, you are hosting a celebration in a neighborhood park. Hold it directly after school lets out. In other words, if school ends at 3:00 pm, start the party at 3:00 pm. You could lose parents who don't want to wait around with unruly kids or you will have kids just arrive early. Be ready at 3:00 pm. Hire a game truck or create a carnival-like atmosphere. Have a DJ there spinning some tunes to keep it lively. You could do similar things as the Food Truck Frenzy and have a spray tattoo artist or face painter. Keep in mind that a spray tattoo artist can do a TON of tattoos in an hour. A good face painter can only do a single digit number in an hour.

Many of those food truck vendors might come in handy for this event. Perhaps have a cupcake food truck or a gelato/ice cream truck. Some companies will host "sundae bars" where they provide everything for the kids to make their own sundaes. What a treat for the kids! It's not only the last day of school, but the beginning of summer and they get to eat sundaes and play games!

Remind people to bring chairs and blankets to the event. Kids will love to run everywhere and get their pent-up energy out!

For a Back to School Event, try the same type of format. You might even want to partner with a local charity that provides school supplies to kids that need them. What a great way to support the local community at the same time as hosting a fun event.

One of the funniest things I have heard is that parents often request alcohol at these events. They say that they need it to prepare themselves for the summer and at the Back to School event, they are celebrating! I wouldn't necessarily suggest having the alcohol at such a kid-friendly event, but it's amusing.

After hearing that request many times, another idea that I thought might be a good one was a Moms and Mimosas

Event. Maybe host the event at a community center in the neighborhood or somewhere similar. Just simply have mimosas and fruit right after the kids are dropped off at school. I guarantee you would have a lot of parents show up! I know our local coffee shops were almost always Standing Room Only on the first days of school in my farm! The parents are celebrating!

Host a Santa and Mrs. Claus Event

I loved hosting this event. Particularly when my daughter was young and still "believed". Afterwards, it was still fun, and she loved being involved in the event to help the younger kids continue to believe.

I always hosted this event in my own home. It was easier to control and to be honest, it just had a more "holiday" feel because I loved (still do) to decorate for Christmas! The key for this event is to book it early and to get a really good Santa and Mrs. Claus. Luckily, ours was amazing. They never broke character. To this day, if I met them on the street out of costume, I wouldn't know who they were, and this was after working with them for years. They were absolutely terrific.

I didn't invite my entire farm to this event. Due to the nature of it, I couldn't have hundreds of people showing up. Instead, I invited my "A" clients and my smaller farm of my own neighborhood. We always had a great turnout.

People arrived and were greeted by myself and my family. Mrs. Claus soon followed. She suggested a great idea. She wanted everyone to have nametags. That way, Mrs. Claus knew who they were right away. The kids didn't think twice about it. I had some printouts of Christmas coloring pages, along with colors on a couple of tables. Kids could sit down and color. I also had Christmas cookies, hot chocolate and water available. Mrs. Claus made the rounds as the kids were waiting to talk to Santa. They loved, loved talking to her and it made their wait time go so much more smoothly.

I put the Big Man in another room by himself. The kids could not see him, but knew he was in there. The key with this entire event was that I never put a time limit on Santa's visit with kids. You might be thinking "Oh wow. What if Suzie talks to him for thirty minutes?". Yep, that happened. However, what typically happened next was that Johnny was terrified of Santa and only spent the bare minimum of time with him. Kids loved talking to Santa and parents loved that they were not being rushed out of there. Mrs. Claus played a key part in this process, too. Since she knew the kids' names, she would bring them into see Santa and say "Papa, you remember Suzie, right? You won't believe what she has been up to!". If we had time, we even asked the parents to jot down something that they wanted Santa to tell the kids. Mrs. Claus made sure to give that to him before she brought the kids inside with the parents. Many times, it was something like "Tell Joey that he needs to improve that math grade," or "Tell Suzie to be nicer to her brother Matt". Parents loved it!

Our final touch was that we took photos of Santa and the kids. We also often took photos of the kids with Mrs. Claus. They just loved her and wanted photos with her, too. After the event, we emailed the photos to each person. The event was always held in November, so we could get the photos to the parents in time for holiday cards. We often received a lot of cards with our photos on them! Parents also posted them in on social media and thanked us for the event. Other people would post comments asking where the event was held, wanting more information. It was great publicity for us. We in turn would post photos, videos, etc. on our social media. Again, another event with a lot of good will and free publicity, too!

Distribute Thanksgiving Pies

Okay, this is not a novel idea. I know many agents that host this event every year. However, when I teach my farming class, it's rare that more than one person has heard of it!

This was one of my favorites farming events. It was also one of my most successful events. I was skeptical when I first started doing it but had heard so many good things about the event from other agents in other parts of the country. I had to try it.

At the beginning of every November, I would mail out postcards to my past clients, to my small neighborhood farm and to really strong prospects. I would say something about being thankful for all of our clients, neighbors and friends at this time of year. In gratitude, I offered to provide a free Thanksgiving pie to them. They just needed to pick the kind – apple or pumpkin! They could sign up on our website, call me or email me. I then sent out a reminder email and phone call. The touch points for these groups of people were off the charts. These are people that I really wanted to touch, too. Their responses also provided me updated emails and phone numbers.

Once I knew how many apple and pumpkin pies were needed, I ordered them from my local Sam's Club. Costco or other bakeries would work, too. I know an agent who bakes the pies! Not only are pies not my expertise, I couldn't imagine baking a multitude of them. It was safer to order them.

I always held this event on the Monday or Tuesday afternoon before Thanksgiving. The beauty of it was that your farm comes to you – you are not out delivering pies for days! I would rent out the community center in the farm, decorate it for Thanksgiving and have my farm come there to pick the pies up. You could also host it in your office's conference room. You could be available all day that way.

By the way, I always created a sticker to put on the pie. Something similar to the postcard, but I made sure my contact info was on it. Many times, these pies were going to be seen by a lot of other friends and family of my farm. I heard that many people said "Wow, your real estate agent gave you this pie? What a neat idea. My agent never did that for me!". A conversation about me then ensued. Not bad!

Another idea is to team up with a lender or another vendor to provide hot apple cider or hot chocolate if you want to share the cost. I know an agent that always teams up with her local humane society. She has a pet available for adoption at the event. People start to expect it and can't wait to meet the pet, which always finds a new home at her event.

Why did I love this event so much? For three reasons. One, people came to this event that never came or responded to anything else. To this day, I have no idea why. I often joked that they would drive by three Sam's Clubs to get their free pie. Two, people didn't just run in and pick up a pie. Sure, every now and then one of them would send their son or daughter in to pick up the pie and they would run out. Overall, that was the minority. Most of the people came in and were relaxed. They wanted to talk. You know how sometimes you always wonder if a client really put that pond in the backyard or if they really ended up liking being that close to their son's school? This was my time to find out. I loved it. Three, I always obtained business out of it. That was not my focus at all. However, I had people tell me "Karen, I just don't like our house any more" or "I gave my brother your name and number. He needs to buy a house in the next few months." It was just a casual, no pressure event and people loved it.

One last key piece of this event – makes sure your pies are great. Not just good, but great. Sam's Club's pies are just that – they are big, and I don't know how many people could make a better pie. Many clients would tell me that they had a fork in their car or that they were stopping by the grocery store on their way home to pick up a gallon of ice cream or whip cream. I don't think a lot of the pies even made it to Thanksgiving!

Hand Out Fourth of July Pies

This event is identical to the Thanksgiving Pie event, but it's held around July 4th. I always had a hard time doing something in the summer as it was my busiest time business-wise. I didn't want to re-create the wheel, so I started handing out apple pies around July 4th. Before I started hosting this event, I would always regret that I didn't have some type of summer event by the end of August. I was just so busy that it didn't happen. When I started planning this one, it was easy to do, and we were able to hold a summer event.

It became so popular that people started requesting a choice between apple and cherry pies. I didn't even know that cherry pies were so popular!

Some of the same people came to this event as at the Thanksgiving event, but we also had new people who attended. They would comment that they always left town for Thanksgiving and would miss that pie event, so they appreciated the summer event.

We always tried to figure out when people would be off for July 4th. Many companies would give their employees both July 4th and another day off work. We would never hand out pies on those days as we figured people had plans. We tried to do it before the holiday started. Sometimes we were doing it on June 30th if the July 4th holiday landed right after a weekend. That might sound early, but we always had a crowd of people attend.

Valentine's Candy

I wanted to be top of mind with past clients and prospects in February. That's when my listing appointments really started to increase so I wanted to make sure to be in the mix if someone was thinking of selling their home or knew someone thinking about it.

I simply bought a lot of Valentine's Day candy boxes from the local dollar store. Four pieces were in each heart-shaped box. I created a sticker with a corny line on it (i.e. "For a Sweet Deal, call Karen") and placed the sticker on each box. I dropped them off at homes to save on postage and to perhaps see people at the same time.

I also decided to start mailing the boxes to past clients that were now out of state. I always had a hard time figuring out how to stay in touch with those particular clients. I knew that they still had friends and family in Colorado. I wanted to be the agent that they remembered when those friends and family members needed real estate assistance. Did it cost more? Yes, the postage cost more than the dollar box of candy. However, I can tell you that the results were terrific. I always received at least one referral. People were shocked that I took the time to send them a box of chocolates!

Valentine's Flowers

Another Valentine's idea is pretty creative for those people that either forget Valentine's or just don't have or want to spend the money.

Host a Valentine's Day "I Forgot" event at a local community center, school, etc. For two hours at the end of the day before Valentine's Day, hand out flowers or something similar. The key is to make it easily transferrable as a gift. What does that mean? Think about the husband that forgot to buy anything for his wife on Valentine's. He can stop by and pick up some flowers, put his name on an attached card and then take it home. Voila!

I also think this is a good idea for those people that may not have a sweetheart on Valentine's Day. Someone just divorced, a widow, a single person – you get the drift. Market it to them as well. They can stop by and pick up their own Valentine's Day gift. You could have the card pre-filled.

I know some agents have relationships with florists for closing gifts. Capitalize on that relationship and work out a deal on the flowers!

Mother's Day Flowers

Again, I'm not re-creating the wheel on this one. It's a very similar idea to the Valentine's Day Flowers event. Set it up the same way.

I like this event for Grandmothers who may not have their grandkids nearby, for kids to pick up a gift for their moms and for the fathers that again forget to pick up something for their wives.

Host of Tour of Homes

I absolutely love this idea for farming! This event is a perfect way to showcase your neighborhood expertise. Everyone has neighbors that want to show off their homes. Maybe they just had their kitchen remodeled, maybe they are passionate about decorating, maybe they are just really proud of their home! On the other side of the coin, I would receive requests from homeowners to see a similar house that maybe had a finished basement or remodeled their kitchen. They wanted to get ideas for their own homes. I always laughed when someone would call and ask if I could get them into a home because they saw a contractor there for months and they wanted to see the end result. The house wasn't for sale. I guess that they thought that every real estate agent had a magic key that allowed them entry to every home in the neighborhood!

For this event to work, you need time. Plan it far in advance. Advertise it and ask for volunteers for their homes to be showcased on a "Happy Valley Ranch Tour of Homes". Mention that only "x" number of homes will be selected this year. By doing this you might reduce the disappointment if their home doesn't get selected and you can create the idea that this is an annual event. You may very well want to start doing it on an annual basis if it's a big success. You will want to have a variety of homes on the tour, too.

Another key with this event is to talk to your attorney. Get a liability waver together and have the homeowners sign it. If someone slips and falls on this tour, it could become a legal nightmare, so you want to have your "t's" crossed and "i's" dotted.

I would also not recommend holding this event at the holidays. Many people want to show off their homes during this time, but there is just so much room for problems. Gifts being stolen, ice on the ground, inclement weather cancelling the event. Hold the tour in the Spring or Summer. Don't play around with the weather. Spring and Summer can also have their own set of problems, but at least you are eliminating the winter weather conditions from the mix.

After securing the homes that will be shown, you will need to come up with a date and make sure that all of the homeowners can make it. Create an area that will be the "staging area" – the pick-up and drop off spot. Maybe have that area at a local community center, school or restaurant. You can have a booth/tent/table set up at the staging area to provide neighborhood information to the tour participants. You could also have snacks available – make it into a party type of atmosphere where people want to talk to you and find out about your business. After all, if they are taking a tour of homes in your farm, they may be interested in that neighborhood or they may be homeowners themselves. You could easily convert them into clients one day!

Rent a van of some sort (preferably a comfortable one and not your Uncle Joe's van that he vacuumed for the occasion) and transport groups of people to the first house. You may need more than one van. Most of the van services can provide a driver for you, too. Start at the first house. You cannot possibly be in numerous places at the same time, so you will need assistance. Someone will need to take the tour participants around the house in an orderly fashion. You don't want people just wandering aimlessly through the home for security reasons. Always have the homeowner present in their own home, too. Having someone guide people through the home and having the homeowner present will encourage homeowners to participate as a "host" of the tour of homes. By doing this, you are easing some fears up front.

You should stay at the pick-up and drop off station to greet people and to answer questions. You will also be monitoring the time it is taking to get through the houses. You may also want to hire a photographer to take photos of the tour homes, people going through the tour and perhaps video parts of it. It's all great advertising for you after the fact. Think about whether you will need the tour participants to sign a waiver allowing you to use their photos and videos for future advertising.

In order to figure out how many people are coming, you could sell tickets and have that money go to a local charity. That prevents just anyone from deciding to get on the van at the last minute and go to the houses. You may also attract the attention of the local media by hosting an event where the proceeds are going to a charity. Not only are you doing a good deed, you are getting some great publicity.

I would also suggest that you provide direction to the homeowner early on. Find out what they want to show off in their home. Some areas may be off limits and you have to determine that early on. You will want to figure out the parade route through each home and then which home will be first, second, etc. Remind the homeowner to put away valuables and anything that they don't want the general public to see. Also, host a tour the night before just for the participating homeowners. They will want to see the other homes themselves and it's a perfect way to get a private tour and not have them leave their own home during the actual tour.

As you can see, this event requires a lot of pre-work and assistance from other people. However, the end result could be spectacular. The tour could truly be an annual event with homeowners anxious to be selected for the tour. Plus, other homeowners and neighbors could look forward to it every year.

Host a Holiday Happy Hour

I just groaned when I typed the words above. Did you hear me? I then smiled. Why? Because my husband, daughter and I hosted a holiday happy hour at our own home for many years. We kind of dreaded it every year, but then would look back and realize that we had a great time.

You certainly don't have to host it at your own home. You could host it at a local restaurant, community center or meeting space. We hosted it at our home because it was already decorated, it was in the farm, it was cheaper than renting out a space and it was just easier to do it that way.

We would invite our surrounding neighbors and past clients. We always enjoyed talking to them and catching up. They in turn would meet other past clients and swap stories. We always obtained business out of this event and we weren't trying. We just wanted an opportunity to talk to these folks.

Our key to success with the party was that we held it on December 23rd. That may seem like a weird date, but it worked. We weren't competing with other parties, people often had December 24th off work and most people were just "done" with the holiday and wanted to relax. Sure, some people didn't attend because they were out of town, but I think more people came than if we held it earlier in the month.

We tried everything from having the party fully catered to doing it all ourselves. We finally found the magic formula that worked for us. We would not make any of the food. We would have it delivered to our home. We would also hire a bartender (she was actually a neighbor's daughter that had worked as a bartender at a local country club) to handle the drinks. Basically, we found that if we were trying to make sure that the food was done or that people had drinks, we never were able to talk to anyone. We also found out that no one wanted desserts. So we ended up with finger food and drinks. That's it. People scarfed the food up and enjoyed just going to get their own drinks.

I have heard that some agents hold these types of events and put together raffle giveaways. They go to the Black Friday sales and purchase things like a big tv or some other electronics. People came to the party to see if they could win. If you proceed with this route, one thing to consider is that you need to be able to say that anyone was invited to this event or you could run into a RESPA violation. Talk to your real estate attorney about it for more details.

The biggest problem with this event was that people never just stayed for an hour. We didn't expect them to, but every year we would have people at our home after midnight. We were pretty exhausted by that point. It's not that we didn't like the people, it was just that we were ready for the party to be over!

Host a Pool Party

If you are a farming a neighborhood with a pool, this could be a great event for you to host. If your farm doesn't have a pool, but there is one nearby, you may be able to rent the pool for a period of time and host a similar party.

Most HOAs will allow a pool to be "rented" for a certain time period. Get on the schedule early. Keep in mind that some pools might require lifeguards to be present and you may have to pay for their time. Don't try to avoid having lifeguards. It's worth the peace of mind to have them there.

Decide what you want to occur during the party. You could rent a movie to play. Many rental companies have screens that they will bring to a pool party, along with the equipment to play the movie. This is a nice event to hold at dusk. People can stay in the pool and watch a movie!

You could grill hot dogs, a snow cone machine, a sundae station – just a few ideas. A DJ is always a nice touch to add to the party atmosphere. You could also have pool games with some cute prizes available. Maybe a diving toss game, a swimming race or a synchronized swimming contest. The sky is the limit as far as ideas.

Of course, you will want to have some type of tent set up with your information in it. You may want to hand out drinks or snacks to get people to come to talk to you. Make sure to walk around and engage with other people throughout the event.

Host a Fall Festival

I know lots of agents who host Fall Festivals in their farms every year. The fact that they do it year after year demonstrates that they are worth doing.

Basically, you will want to host this event in the farm or close to the farm. If you live in an area with winter weather conditions, I would suggest doing it at the end of September or the first week of October at the latest. Plus, people are really getting into the autumn aspect of the season by September.

A Saturday morning always seems to a popular time to host this event. Maybe late morning into the early afternoon. You will probably want to have it in an open field. Buy some hay bales and place them around for the Fall-like atmosphere. Try to find some fake fences and place them at the corner or main entrance to the event. Decorate the area with corn stalks or scarecrows. Scatter some pumpkins around the area.

Bounce houses are very popular at these events. As always, I suggest that you talk to your attorney about liability for injuries etc. Find out if the bounce house company will have attendants present. Yes, they cost more but it can be so worth it as they are monitoring how many people are in the houses, if too much rough horse play is going on, etc.

Perhaps have a face painter, a balloon maker or a spray tattoo artist. If you expect a large turnout, make sure that you have more than one of each of these vendors, so people don't get fed up with super long lines. Lines are okay as long as they aren't ridiculous. It also gives you time to walk down them and talk to people.

Again, a DJ or band is a great idea. I know plenty of agents who have a live band at these events. It could be a great way to engage your farm. Advertise that the Fall Festival is occurring on "x" date and that you are looking for a local band. You might be surprised at the feedback. You may end up having to go somewhere to hear them but believe me it's worth it. You don't want to hire a band who you think plays cover tunes to find out that they play cover tunes of death metal. Do your homework! Maybe ask for a video of them playing if you can't see them live. Hiring a band from the farm is another way to show that you are "all in" with the neighborhood.

If you really want to go all out, you could have a midway

of sorts with games. Many companies are out there that provide all of this to you, at a cost of course. It's just another way to keep people at the Fall Festival. You will want homeowners to want to be there and want to stay.

Food? In the morning, you could serve donuts and coffee. If you are there during lunch, you could have hot dogs grilling or a couple of food trucks available. Make sure to have some desserts available – maybe cupcakes, cotton candy, bobbing for apples.

A pumpkin giveaway is another popular feature in a Fall Festival. I know from experience that you will want to monitor this one carefully. I suggest having lots of pumpkins available. However, I would place them in some contained area, so you can keep an eye on them. Better yet, have someone in charge of the entire pumpkin patch. By contained area, I am referring to maybe putting some fake fences around the pumpkins. Why? I have been to Fall Festivals in which people arrive with wagons. They put numerous pumpkins in them. They just walk off with them. If asked, they will say that they are getting some for neighbors. Also, people just driving by (and don't live anywhere near the farm) will stop by and pick up free pumpkins. Believe me, when word gets out that free pumpkins are available, the whole city will find out and show up. Maybe have a pumpkin limit. People who live in the farm often get very angry that people who don't live in the neighborhood are taking the pumpkins and will come to complain to you. Those are just not conversations that you want to have so plan in advance. At the end of the day, nothing says Fall like pumpkins, so I think the hassle is totally worth having them available.

If you don't want to foot the bill for this entire event, you could probably easily have vendors chip in. Try a local insurance agent. He/she may be willing to pay for the face painters if you let him/her have a tent at the event. Pet sitters, house cleaners, plumbers, roofers, you name it. Anyone associated with housing would be the first groups of people that I would approach about helping to subsidize the cost.

Don't forget yourself. Make sure to advertise your name prominently. Have a big tent at the entrance. Hand out real estate information, but also something that attendees might need such as water bottles.

Hold a Holiday Lights Contest

I hosted this type of contest for several years. It became so popular that the HOA took it over. It was a great event and had many positives, but there was one negative that I will let you know about.

Basically, I advertised the contest beginning in November, even late October as in Colorado many people would put up their lights in that timeframe to beat the weather. A weekend with seventy-degree weather in November? People hung their lights because they knew the next weekend could see below-zero temperatures. I wanted to provide people with enough advance notice that they could add a little pizazz to their lights if they so desired.

I would advertise that people needed to sign up to participate. You could have them do that in a variety of ways – phone calls to you, emails, sign up on your website. If you have the capability, you could have a map created with their homes listed on it and put it on your website. You could advertise the participants, so people would go to your website to find some good houses to look at during "light looking" nights.

Our prizes were simply gift certificates to the home improvement stores to help them stock up on more lights for the next year. I truly believe that people didn't enter for that gift card. They wanted the recognition. What they really loved was that I would put a big sign in their yard announcing that they were the Holiday Lights winner for the neighborhood. Of course, my logo and information were also on the sign. People loved having the signs in their yards. They didn't want me to take them out!

I made sure to have the contest about a week or so before Christmas. I wanted my signs in their yards for prime-time light viewing. Plus, many people go out of town and I wanted them to know if they won the contest.

As for picking winners, here's where the words of caution are going to appear. Never, ever – again, never, ever – be the judge of this contest. You just don't want that pain and heartache. I always asked local lenders or title company reps to be the judges. I also reminded the participants as to when the light contest would be held. It never failed that one or two houses would not have their lights on and would ask us to come back later. Getting the judges in a car at a specific time on a specific date during the holidays was hard enough once. I just couldn't come back by later. I reminded and reminded the participants again before the contest about the judging date, so I didn't feel too badly about not coming back. However, no matter what happened, I always had unhappy participants. I always received calls the day the winners were announced. Other participants wanted to know why they weren't chosen. Were we against religion because their house had a cross on it? Were we only wanting religious houses because crosses were on the winners? The list goes on and on. You can't win so try to reduce the complaints by not being a judge yourself. Make sure that you let participants know that you are not the judge, but that you have local vendors from "XYZ" mortgage company, etc. judging. To protect those judges, I wouldn't say who they were unless they want the advertising themselves. They probably won't!

I would also suggest having more than one winner. Maybe have a first and second place winner. Or a "Most Creative" winner along with "Overall Winner". You can come up with your own captions. It helps to have more than one winner and sometimes one house fits one category more than another. Plus, don't forget your signs are up in more than one yard!

Host a Re-Gift New Year's Party

You may be saying to yourself that you have no desire to host a holiday cocktail party, hold a lights contest or hand out pies. The "Re-Gift Party" is an event that is a low-key, but fun.

The premise is that everyone brings a gift that they received that they just don't want. They basically want to re-gift it. They wrap it up (in any kind of wrapping paper – birthday, Christmas) and bring it to the party. You could have it at your home if you would like to keep the costs down.

Perhaps hold the party as a pot-luck. People each bring a dish. You could have them bring a dish that they really wanted during the holidays, but no one served it. I would suggest having some drinks available, but you could even have a BYOB (Bring Your Own Bottle) party. Kind of a "I'm over the holidays" and "I want to now get what I want" party. It can be a lot of fun!

Invite some of the farm, past clients, etc. You could advertise it saying it's low-key and it's a recuperation type of party. People will love it.

Chapter 9

Resources

I have provided you with lots of ideas of things to do to farm a neighborhood. At this point, many people ask if I sleep at night or how I created the marketing pieces. Yes, I do sleep, and I have found easy, less-expensive ways to create marketing materials. Keep in mind that I just listed a ton of ideas, but I didn't do them all in one year.

I pace things out throughout the year. As I mentioned earlier in the book, at the end of each year, I plan for the next year. I plan events, mailings and the costs of doing each of them. I also have a system set up in which I can outline what I need to do get an event done. For instance, the July 4th pies. If I didn't plan in advance for that event, it just wouldn't happen as that was my busiest real estate season. Instead, I reserved a space to hold the event in March. In April, I created a postcard for the event. In May, I put together a mailing list. In June, I mailed the postcards and also set up two emails to go out to remind people of the event. I piecemealed the project to make it do-able. It went off without a hitch.

As for marketing, you need to do what works for you. I know lots of agents who hire graphic designers to create marketing pieces, others hire high school students to create the pieces, some agents use virtual assistants to do their marketing and others have someone on their staff that does them. I ended up doing my own. No, I was not the best out there. However, I knew myself well enough to know that I was pretty picky. I am not good at describing what I want, but I know what I don't want. I can look at something and say "Oh, that's not what I wanted. I need it to look jazzier and brighter." However, every time that I would send something back to the graphic designer, it would cost me money.

As of this writing, I am using a website called www.Canva.com to create my marketing pieces. I love it. It's like it's a graphic design program for the non-graphic designer. Both a free and paid version are available. Canva allows me to play around with the marketing pieces until I get what I want. I don't work for them, I just love using the program. It changes almost daily so by the time you read this, it could be in a different format than today.

I also really believe in using the Every Door Direct Mail (EDDM) system through the United States Postal Service. It's just so much cheaper to mail a marketing piece through the EDDM system and you can use very unique sizes to stand out. Most online printers have programs set up just for

EDDM.

Chapter 10

Summary

At this point, you have probably realized that I am a Farming Nerd to the one millionth degree. I built my very successful real estate business on it and know it works. For my business, farming helped me weather a major downward turn in the market and the upward turn back in the market. We all know that the economy changes regularly, and farming is a way to have consistent business throughout any economic change.

Yes, my head has been turned by internet leads, by door knocking, by for sale by owners – the list goes on. As I have said throughout this book, combining any of those programs with farming could be very successful for you. You just don't have to do them all. Find what works for you, what fits your personality and lifestyle and just do it!

Good luck!

***

Thanks so much for reading this book. Hopefully, you are walking away with some new ideas to obtain clients for your real estate business.

As you probably can tell, I am passionate about farming, along with helping agents create systems to run to their business, creating a team that fits their business, helping them create amazing customer service for their clients and also helping agents learn how to treat their business like a business. I offer online classes along with teaching them in person. If interested in bringing a class to your area, simply reach out to me on my website – www.freshideastraining.com.

I also love coaching agents. Nothing makes my day brighter than to help an agent increase their business along with balancing their work/life. Since I was actually a high-producing agent, I feel like I bring a lot to the table. I know what it's like to be an agent. I'm not simply telling an agent that they should do a certain thing without ever having sold real estate. I lived that life for many years so I "get it". If you need further coaching information, simply contact me through the website – www.freshideastraining.com – and I will send you some information.

Last, but not least, if you have found this book helpful, I would appreciate a quick review on Amazon.com! The reviews mean a lot to me personally and also to the Amazon Gods. Simply go to www.amazon.com and search for this book and leave a quick review!

Thanks again for reading!

Made in the USA
Coppell, TX
27 February 2020